After You

After You

Letters of Love, and Loss,
to a Husband and Father

NATASCHA McELHONE

VIKING
an imprint of
PENGUIN BOOKS

VIKING

Published by the Penguin Group
Penguin Books Ltd, 80 Strand, London WC2R ORL, England
Penguin Group (USA) Inc., 375 Hudson Street, New York, New York 10014, USA
Penguin Group (Canada), 90 Eglinton Avenue East, Suite 700, Toronto, Ontario, Canada M4P 2Y3
(a division of Pearson Penguin Canada Inc.)
Penguin Ireland, 25 St Stephen's Green, Dublin 2, Ireland (a division of Penguin Books Ltd)
Penguin Group (Australia), 250 Camberwell Road, Camberwell, Victoria 3124, Australia
(a division of Pearson Australia Group Pty Ltd)
Penguin Books India Pvt Ltd, 11 Community Centre, Panchsheel Park, New Delhi – 110 017, India
Penguin Group (NZ), 67 Apollo Drive, Rosedale, North Shore 0632, New Zealand
(a division of Pearson New Zealand Ltd)
Penguin Books (South Africa) (Pty) Ltd, 24 Sturdee Avenue, Rosebank, Johannesburg 2196,
South Africa

Penguin Books Ltd, Registered Offices: 80 Strand, London WC2R ORL, England

www.penguin.com

First published 2010
1

The acknowledgements on page 113 constitute an extension of this copyright page

Set in 11/13 pt Bembo Book MT Std
Typeset by TexTech International
Printed in Great Britain by Clays Ltd, St Ives plc

A CIP catalogue record for this book is available from the British Library

ISBN: 978-0-670-91909-3

www.greenpenguin.co.uk

To my three cubs, you are above and beyond anything
I could have wished for. Your Dadu would
be so very proud of you.

To my mother and Roy – for showing
me what love is.

Preface

26th November 2009

My husband died suddenly eighteen months ago from a heart attack. He was at home. I was away working in Los Angeles with our two sons and I was pregnant with our third.

It has been an extraordinary eighteen months. I never believed I would say this, but at the moment I feel some happiness. I don't understand why – I loved him so completely – how can I possibly be happy without him? And yet somehow he has become a part of us, we have expanded, stretched, as a result of his death. We have reached for the furthest corners of ourselves and been surprised. No one has replaced him, no one has filled that void, but I think we are growing into its place.

When I was told my husband was dead, it was how I imagine war to be. Carnage, limbs being torn off, flesh left flapping in the wind. To come from that feeling to this now seems impossible; I don't know how it has happened. All I can think is that we humans are irrepressible; this hunger to live, to thrive, overwhelms every other impulse.

I am lucky I have these three juggernauts of love in my life who stop for nothing, who live here right now and have taught me to do the same. These little boys are my teachers, even Baby twisting his head to one side with a wry smile to grab my attention and snap me out of any reverie. There's little time for reflection in our new world; it's a 'doing', 'going places', hungry world packed with questions, most of which I can't answer.

What brings a lump to my throat now is not having someone to share all this with. When the time comes and I proudly watch these three boys become men setting out on their own journeys – three sets of broad shoulders disappearing, carving a way towards their own destiny. Not having HIM there to celebrate that with . . . I can't even write it . . .

I hate that he will never see who they become, that they will never have the chance to show him.

★

I hope one day my boys will be glad to have a record of this.
What is the sense in loss if in its place it brings nothing?

Writing this has been a scaffolding to help prop me up, a handrail as I take my first steps down this dark, lonely staircase. Maybe it can be the same for someone else who has lost their person, their love?

I have found great comfort in two books, A Grief Observed *by C. S. Lewis and* Living On A Seabed *by Lindsay Nicholson. Thank you to these authors and the many people who have helped me over the last eighteen months.*

Martin's death is the closest I have come to death myself. Coming back from that brings a new lease of life, a belief (however fleeting) that I must quickly share these experiences before they evaporate.

What follows are just snippets of my thoughts and feelings chased across a page in bed at 2 a.m., in a supermarket queue, at a school gate, even whilst giving birth. Writing to my husband has enabled me to keep him here long enough to 'come to terms' with losing him. So here it is, my catharsis, my medicine, my prescription . . .

'You know, I'm a doctor and I can tell you that the heart is the strongest muscle in the body. No matter how much damage it takes, it always repairs itself.'

Martin Kelly

March 2009

I am going through my diaries since you have died, all the things I have written to and about you. This strange exercise of 'writing', which I resisted at first, has now become like breathing for me, essential, if I am to accept what has happened.

I had a message on my phone from you as I watched our boys in their gymnastics class. Otis I remember was excelling in 'basket' position; Theo, long-limbed and colty, was bounding across a crash mat. I had an unexpected hiatus in my day. I was filming at the studio opposite and had a break whilst they shot a different sequence. I listened to one of the many beautiful messages from you, Martin, 'Monkey', so many different names I gave you. You loved me, missed me, you couldn't wait to see me again and kiss my pregnant bump, escape for a night to a romantic hideaway for our tenth wedding anniversary. You would tumble about with the boys on the beach for a few days before going back to the coalface in London. There were only nine more days until we would see each other; everything was booked and written in stone. I deleted the message because there would always be more messages like that from you. The next message was from your best friend, Neil. He sounded low, dark, he wanted me to call him. It was too late UK time, but I thought maybe he had had a crisis with his girlfriend and needed to talk. No, I won't call him back – it's too late. Hmm . . . there's a monkey on my shoulder saying I should. Why? Instinctively I walk towards the exit and dial Neil's number –

'Are you alone?' he says.

'Well, -ish, don't worry,' I say. 'Fire away.'

'They did everything they could,' he says.

'Right, what are you talking about?'

'Everyone tried their best,' he says.

'I have no idea what you're talking about. Monkey, are you talking about Monkey? Neil, what's happened, is there something wrong?'

'*Everyone did everything,*' he says.

'*What the fuck, what the fuck are you trying to tell me? I don't under-stand you, are you trying to tell me he's not well, something has hap-pened?*'

'*Yes – he – they tried everything . . .*'

'*Neil, don't do this, don't fucking do this, you're kidding me, he's he's not dead?*'

I suggest this ridiculous idea for him to refute, so things can improve, we can get back on track, get to the bottom of what's really going on.

'*Yes, he didn't make it.*'

'*Make what? What the fuck?*' I wail.

My knees fold underneath me, this stupid phone slips from my hand. Two women whom I barely know run towards me, one of them sobbing. They've been standing watching me as I head towards my trailer from the kids' gym, knowing what I'm hearing on the phone. We're in a fucking movie – there's trailers everywhere – those women were just perfect in that scene. Yes, when you're really '*in the moment*' your body does strange things – my legs went to jelly.

No, no, snap back. We're not making that kind of movie, something just happened, I have no idea what, let me pick up the phone, let me call him back.

I had a dream like this last week, just like this – my love, you, had died, I was in LA working and after you died I carried on working. Yes, that's all it is, except my dream went further into it than this. I'll call back, I lost the thread; I didn't get the whole picture. Up the metal steps, into that transient space where I wait to act, let me in there, the comfort of that squishy carpet and Formica, it's familiar; this blazing sun is making things swirl. Into that trailer with its tin-can walls and door that closes, then I can think.

'*Nancy, run and get my kids, will you? Their class is finishing, they'll wonder where I am.*'

'*Yes, yes, what shall I do or say, where shall I take them?*'

'*Kitchen, hot chocolate, I'll call you, I have to make a phone call.*'

She's sobbing, wiping her nose, giving me '*brave*', finding a smile some-where in her arsenal, something good to leave me with.

There's a teamster there, like a rock. I think she's sitting on the sofa in my trailer; I can't be totally sure. Who is she? She seems to know everything, she's seen this before, nothing is surprising her. Maybe if I look at her long enough I'll understand too . . . No, I'll ask her if she can leave.

'Erm, I have to make a call.'

She has a strong American accent. 'You want me to go?'

'Yes, please, is that okay? You're very kind.'

What the fuck am I doing? Come on, call him back, get the fuck alone, she'll understand, quick.

She leaves.

Maybe I should call Monkey and see what he thinks is going on? Well, his phone might be off, apparently he might not be able to answer a phone any more, oh, for god's sake, of course he can, he just left me a message – Neil's was straight after – he'll still have his phone.

I'll call Neil, just redial.

'WHAT – what the fuck is going on?'

'Tash, he didn't make it. Everyone –'

'No everyone, no everyone! Is he dead? Are you trying to tell me he's dead?'

'Yes, he's dead.'

'No, no, no, that's just not possible, it's impossible, isn't it?'

'Yes, it's impossible, he didn't make it, everyone –'

'What happened? What happened, tell me tell me.'

'Heart, heart attack. Adam was amazing, found him, tried, everyone tried their best.'

'Why do you keep saying that? Don't do this, this can't be, he can't be, how do you know? Is he really dead already now? Where is he?'

'He's in the –'

I cut him off. 'I have to go, I have to see the boys.'

Through my window, I see one running, the other chasing him, ice cream trickling down their wrists. Otis squeals ''Top it, Beanie!' They are ushered towards the door.

Let's go back, let's go back to five minutes ago when we knew nothing, when there was no inkling, when I was the happiest fullest woman in the world.

I'm about to smash everything, I can't do this to them. Fuck fuck fuck,

I wipe some tears from my face – I don't want to scare them. Theo steps up first, Otis struggles, panting with the reach of each step.

Theo looks up at me and gasps, shit, he's never seen me cry, fuck can you believe that? I've never had a reason to cry in front of him.

'Mummy, what's wrong?'

'Come in, come in, close the door. I've got to talk to you. Let's sit down.' We sit in a tight circle, facing one another.

'I've got something horrible to tell you.'

Theo: 'I know what it is – you've lost your job.'

Fuck, I wish. Right now, I wish he was right and that was it.

'No, baby, I wish that was it . . . Dadu's died.'

I held it together for that statement, then the walls of my eyes came tumbling down again. He wails; the little one watches him like a hawk, scanning his big brother's reaction before deciding what his own should be. I watch them too, trying to hold their hands through this, desperate for nothing to go unnoticed, desperate to become two people, split myself in half, like a worm, just grow another body, be everything they need. They melt into my arms, keening, yes – just like giving birth, death is an unfamiliar wail; we're all doing it. Theo stops abruptly, as does Otis.

'But, Mummy, it's not possible. This happens in books, it doesn't happen to me.'

'I know, my love, I know.'

'Are you sure? How do you know?'

'Neil told me, he's had a heart attack.'

'But Dadu was healthy, he was the fittest dad.'

'I know.'

We talked and talked. They said extraordinary things. I've written them down separately if they want to read them one day.

'Do you want to speak to Neil?' I asked.

We called him back.

Theo spoke to him – I can't remember what he said as I was talking to Otis. Pam came into the trailer, also in shock, and hugged them both. After Theo had finished on the phone to Neil, she started talking to him. She's a brilliant mother of her own three girls and I knew I could trust her to talk to him and let him talk.

The three of us moved around the trailer in a series of seated positions. I think I'd remained on the floor throughout, but occasionally I scooted along the carpet to embrace someone, or get close enough to stroke a face. The boys climbed up on to the sofa or slipped on to an arm of it, looking at their incomprehensible world from a different vantage point.

I called my parents, my stepfather, well, father really, answered the phone blearily. It must have been about 2 a.m. for them by now.

I started sobbing before I could speak.

'It's me . . .'

'What is it? What's wrong?'

'Monkey's dead.'

A tidal change in the voice at the other end, repositioning his body presumably to take the full force of this shock, this bullet. I heard my mother asking what was going on in the background. He repeated the news, replacing my nickname with 'Martin' instead.

'I don't understand, Tashy. What's going on? What happened?'

Again, I can't remember much more than that. It trailed on, but once the news was out you sort of departed from the other person for a while as they orbited away from you to assimilate this ridiculous information.

I then called my brother. Pam was still talking to Theo and Otis, beautiful calming words. They all broke into laughter once or twice too, reminiscing about M already.

Answerphone, fuck. I leave a tearful message. Well, not tearful, throat constricted and possibly confused.

'Ip [another ridiculous nickname I concocted years ago], it's me, can you call me back?'

The phone rang fairly instantly. It was him. He was at work and had taken a quick tea break to check his messages and had found the unusual from me.

'Tash, it's me. What is it?'

'Monkey, he's dead.'

'What – what – what the . . . what are you talking about?'

'He died of a heart attack.'

'Hold on, where are you, are you at work?'

'Yes . . .' I think I trailed off into suppressed sobs at this point.

'I'm coming.'

We hung up. Nothing needed saying – he's my brother, he knew.

I've just read this back. God, I hate it, this stream of drivel, this quest for drama – that's what it suddenly feels like. I haven't captured the truth, because the truth was remarkably simple in so many ways. This is a simple thing: your husband, the love of your life, father to your babies, dies. It happens all over the world, every day, in worse circumstances.

Am I putting this down as an additional catharsis? To bring you back to life or to finally say goodbye?

I'm going through a period of slightly pretending this hasn't happened, of trying to make life complete and normal, even projecting what I feel for you on to other people.

I'm going to go back to the diary I kept, well, those sort of bulletin letters I wrote to you, rather than my current thoughts. The diary is immediate, unadulterated somehow. This attempt at a flashback is too exhausting. It's horrible and reads like a sequence of events, rather than the simple implosion of you being gone.

There is no finding you again, but I feel the need to record this, what happened, how it was. If my diaries get lost or burnt, there'll be something on this machine, even if none of us ever wants to read it back.

PART ONE
2008

The first entry is only this:

20th May

My angel dies.

What the hell is that? It looks like a joke, the first line of a song perhaps, something a child might lisp in a Nativity play. How did I even have the nerve to write it?

22nd May

Theo had asked me not to cry in front of him and I really want to honour that. I feel it must be very important for him right now. I didn't manage it this time.

I was packing to go back home to arrange your funeral.

I found your favourite baseball cap in amongst my things, and that was it. My throat swells and tears spring out of me all over again.

Finding your trainers in the back of the car earlier was the same. I had to shove them into Matthew's hands, trying desperately not to crumple into smithereens beside the stinking garbage cans in the driveway. He, my amazing friend, just took them and they disappeared like you.

Anyway it was your cap this time, that thing you look for in a crowd to identify 'your person'. How was the cap here without you? As I was trying not to implode, Theo had walked into my bedroom:

'Mummy, what is it? Don't worry, I've just finished my maths homework.'

'No, my love, [I think I managed to laugh] it's not to do with your maths homework.'

'Well, what is it then?'

'You know.'

He placed his hands on his tiny hips. 'It's Dadu, isn't it? Mummy, I've told you, we've got to move on.'

'I am sure I will, but you see it will take time. I just saw Dadu's cap and it made me sad.'

'Well, shall we rip it up?'

'No.'

'Shall I have it?'

'Yes, if you'd like it, that's a good idea.'

Theo then put the cap on and strutted around the room doing an impersonation of you (the first time I have seen him do that) which made me howl with laughter.

I hope this is the last time he ever feels a need 'to cheer me up'.

What an angel that boy is . . .

About 24th May

Can't remember the date. Found this on scraps of paper:

Back in London, our house is like an election campaign room, a polling station or something. I dragged out every file you had and laid all the paperwork I needed across the floor as there was no room left on the table. Eventually it stretched from one end of the kitchen to the other side of the sitting room floor. How can this side of dying be so complicated? Or is it like that for a reason, so you have no choice but to keep going until you've sorted everything? I never will, this is unsortable, impossible, impossible. My love, thank god you didn't have to do this for me. I'm SO impressed with you all over again, your brain, your planet-sized organised brain.

Me, bedraggled in a nightdress, eating leftovers for breakfast. The boys, sparky, inquisitive, allowed to do most things . . . Suzy and Stephen, Aoife, Jackie – everyone round with pots of food and help, god, I'm lucky. Don't think anyone can help, help implies the situation might improve – without you, what room is there for improvement? Can't clear my head. Parents, Neil, everyone in shock, terrible, horrible shock, but busy, none of us stop.

Your mum wants jobs, always thinking, *What can I do to help?* She has lent money to me – please don't worry, can pay her back very soon.

'to do' list

Get a solicitor
Pension scheme/ cross chk w spiro Bentley
Call jo/nat west
Propose Heal plug to Simon
Call PR co. get exact ingredients from chemist & collette
Sarah DJ to print funeral cards
Rem boys' epitaphs
Mirella's pic of him w boys
Pic of us holding hands – find
Write letter to him, put in his coffin w cds, book, boys' fav
    pokemon cards
Undertakers w Theo – wicker coffin?
Call MDU
Transfer all pics & footage on video to dvds
Camera mem card to Charlie
Call wilts council
SAG – any help?
Cancel his premiums, standing orders
Call Norwich U, dbl chk
Any life policy LPSA?
NHS pension?
Send email re subletting house?
Solic needs do probate
K & C – Neil do death cert.

Call orig mortgage broker
LPSA he paid 70k for directors loan – expln cash flow prob
Find out if I liable for more
tax ref no.
claim otis child benefit

16th June

We did the funeral with your sisters, mother, our boys, Adam, Norman, Ben and Neil, I think. Yes, I think that was it. The boys were mischievous. Theo chose your coffin. What are you doing in a fucking coffin? What the hell is happening? It stayed closed – someone's little fingers tried to prise it open, I distracted him. I didn't look either – you're here in my head; I don't need to see death's version of you.

It was right, just immediate family and your 'brothers'. I know that was enough, as much as the boys could absorb, it's them that have lost – they've lost their dad, this is them saying goodbye to you; that's all that matters.

Then after returning to LA to carry on working I realised it wasn't enough – the rest of us hadn't 'celebrated' you. I hadn't given you the proper send off. People needed to say goodbye; our friends didn't know where to put themselves or what to do. They said they met up and wandered around together in the days following, expecting you to suddenly join in, laughing. But they needed more. I agreed.

My producer, Lou, let me come back to London for a few days. They squeezed my work in either side of the trip. I came on my own this time, the glorious godmothers and my brother took over the boys in LA. I think I returned to London Thurs a.m. and came back to LA Sat a.m. I packed a lot in – actually I didn't sleep. Anyway, you were there that night somehow – it was like one of our really great dinner parties – it started at 6 p.m. and went on till 4 a.m . . .

★

I have to keep in touch with your mum – will email her the poem Adam wrote about you for your wake. She just couldn't face it again – the funeral with our pups was enough for her. Everyone said such incredible things about you, stood around your graveside in the gentle rain. I wish you'd been there to listen to it all. I made a little film about you that ran on a loop at the top of the house throughout the evening. That night went on till 4 a.m.! The boys watched the film as soon as I came back to LA again. They love it; it'll go in their memory boxes of you. Thank god it was Adam that found you dead, thank god he could try everything to make you live again . . . Here's his poem:

Martin

You are a terrible friend.
In scrubs you look the part;
I look like the cleaner.
You are a terrible friend.

Your smile is huge,
especially that extra huge smile.
You fill the room.
You make us all feel safe.

You make me laugh when I should be serious,
you grab my collar when I am frustrated by managers,
you play guitar and paint and sing and run,
you win at tennis,
and speak languages.
My god, you really are a terrible friend.

My wife thinks you are the perfect 'Dadu'.
When things go wobbly, you pause and ruminate and solutions find,
and life seems safe again.

To your questions I give wrong answers.
You pretend that they are right.

You are shy;
you undersell your wondrous talents.
We have to shout about our small victories,
but you keep yours tucked away.

You never meant to make us feel this inadequate.
You are a terrible friend.

When you visit the box that is our life, the light shines bright
    and warm.

My secretary says you smell nice.

You make Natascha's smile as big as yours, you tumble with the boys.
You make sisters laugh and wonder and faint.
You spoil your Mama; her silent pride reaches into my soul.
You are a terrible friend.

Does your watch work on a different time to mine?
It must; you have more hours in your day.
It gives you time to tend to wounded faces, and hearts and lives.
Your fingers place tiny stitches and your arms can cut down trees.

But now you rest at last, a quiet, deep and neat sleep.

From that sudden shock and stark shudder of anguish, you still
    grasp us all,
and bind us in this new ragbag family.

You still thrill us with your electric touch,
and from the stunned paralysis of going
have infected us with a new way to live our lives.

Your vortex has flung us to places we would have never gone.
You have made me write poetry.

Your firm and warm and solid,
smiling,
chuckling,
thrilling power brings joy to me even now.

What a brilliant and delicious feast of a boy you are, Martin.
You really are the most terrible friend.   xxx

16th June contd.

I don't know where to begin about all this; it's too much, but I
have to begin. I've been avoiding writing for three weeks now.
I did write a splurge of love or a tribute, or a confused ramble a
couple of nights after you died in lieu of someone's more dispas-
sionate obituary – but there are so few words that I could ever find
to express what's happened . . .

18th June

. . . I had to stop there as I was called to set. I'm avoiding writing
even though it's usually such a form of release for me and ends up
keeping me focused and resolving or at least airing inexplicable
feelings.

   If I really write, you know, how I feel, then I know this tide of
tears will be unleashed and I don't want to live in that place right
now, there just isn't time for tears. One thing I can do or must get
around to doing: compile a book of all the boys' thoughts, what
they have said to me since it happened.

   Feelings are so transient sometimes, particularly now, and they
change their colours so regularly. I don't necessarily want to record

everything and be bound to it for myself or for them. Perhaps some of this should be forgotten – no, not forgotten, just not remembered.

Nothing I can write reflects or matches up to how I feel. I haven't tried properly yet. I'm not sure about this whilst I'm in a practical, organisational mode. Can I plunge myself into despair and bereavement? Is it important 'to grieve'? Or would grief naturally keep hiccupping its way back through, playing havoc with me, no matter how much I tried to avoid it?

19th June

I realise the only way I'm going to ramp myself up to this, the impossibility of looking at what has happened, is by checking in every day and scribbling something, facing it – I'll just write anything down.

I'm still sleeping very sporadically. Last night I managed six hours though, so at least my driving is safer . . . I'm terrified of that, can you imagine?

> When sorrows come, they come not single spies
> But in battalions.

I can, I really can imagine all that horror now. Something happening to the boys . . . I couldn't cope. You could throw anything at me but not that. Without them there's nothing, nothing exists, there would just be nothing any more.

I'm sure this motivation and strength I feel right now is a desire to be double whatever I was before. Would that help, would they then lose less from not having you?

I can't bear that they are no longer receiving those infusions of love from you and that our unborn baby never will. I know how to talk myself out of any negative spin; I am an optimist. I don't need to do that here – the point of this writing to you, this letter to you, is to be with you, to tell you everything. To tell you how it is without you, what you are missing, how I am missing you, to delve into the shadows, to look at the hopelessness I sometimes feel. I don't want to expose the boys to that. This place I find with you might help shelter them from some of the harder blows I feel. I don't know, I don't know anything. Writing this down feels necessary, whatever it is.

At the moment, whenever I think of you, I see you smiling. You are calm, smooth, buttery and sensual. I see you as eternally healthy, shiny and youthful like some cheesy emancipated yoga teacher. (I know that would make you laugh.) I don't see pain, just good fortune, happiness even. I love you so so much. I know I can cope and I'll try to remain strong but there's still this . . .

A light has gone out in the centre of the room. Anything from here is drawn from my perspective, my memory of you. Yes, I can reach and put a light back on; I can 'realise' you. I would be manipulating the image though, like a projectionist. I am making it all happen, there are no surprises, it's merely my impression of you; nothing new can unfold. That's what death is, the end of change.

I can and do conjure you up in my mind all the time, but that's all it is: 'conjuring', imagining hard, holding you there until you fade and the more I try to hold you the quicker your image fades. It's merely my desperation working hard. It's a world apart from my heart leaping because YOU enter a room. In fact, it's a world apart from anything I know.

The practical stuff – attempting to bring up three boys on my own – that hardly worries me, even though it probably should. Perhaps it's just too overwhelming to think about right now.

I thank god you so often told me what a wonderful mother I was, not because I am but because YOU thought I was.

I know there was no part of you that wanted to die. I feel this strange peace around it sometimes. This feels warm and filling and not the empty void you would imagine after the love of your life dies. Did you know, did I know, I wouldn't be holding your hand into old age? The image of us old together never really glued itself into my mind. I'd imagine it and try to construct it and then it would fade very quickly, too quickly for me to get an impression of it. Ha! There's another retrospective attempt to make sense of it all when sense has no business here. Acceptance and incredulity jammed up against one another – for this moment, acceptance is the winning force.

There's suddenly so much I want to do for and because of you. There is no point in fear or time wasting. I don't know what purpose it served me holding on to those ways of living, but I want to banish them. I want to banish everything that isn't useful; there's no time for it any more. I feel this urge to live at your rhythm, your pace – is it the half of you growing within me? Or perhaps I just can't help it, living for two now, expanding and embracing instead of shrinking inwards which I'm apt to do.

I hope this isn't just a hormone-induced surge of energy. It is this tide, this current that is keeping me afloat, allowing me to give some stability and normality to the boys.

I can't wait to get back home to London and feel you all over the house again. I'll brush past you on stairways, smell you, sense you – a few straggly bits of your aura still trapped in the house. I hope all the windows are closed, so none can escape.

I can't wait to watch all the footage I've never seen of you on your computer. You see, there's a chance to uncover something new about you, to keep you alive for a little bit longer, to eke you out, now that we know the end is here. All those times you could be bothered to pick up the camera when I couldn't, thank god for those. Now we have you in some form – active and alive forever.

Wed 2nd July

Last night lying in bed whilst I am reading them a story, they elect for 'chats' instead of a story and so it begins:

Theo: 'Dying is much worse than breaking your arm or leg, isn't it?'

Me: 'Yes, because you don't recover.'

Theo: 'Well, then the government should give us a disabled parking badge for our car.'

Me: 'But Dadu is dead, he's not disabled.'

Theo: 'Not for *him*, for us; it's very disabling for your father to die, you know.'

Me: 'My angel, you're right, but I don't know if it's physically disabling – i.e. if it stops you walking from the car to your destination.'

He was quiet for a beat and then a huge smile spread across his face, eyes shiny and twinkling.

Theo: 'You know, it's funny you say that but I have actually been walking a bit strange since Dadu died . . .'

I've just had another one of those spectacularly short nights. I always seem to wake after a few hours of sleep, first brain racing and then inevitably I start to drift towards images, your face, your body mostly and then my tears flow. It's the best time for it, my only real time alone to 'grieve' – that expression, that verb, it has a whole new meaning . . .

I don't read or write at the moment. I'm like a vacant robot with sets of tasks or missions to accomplish and that's how life has to be – that is the putting one foot in front of the other for me. It's a strict rota of organising children, loving them, listening to them, bathing them and kissing them, reading to them and showing up to work.

There's the odd hour of stressful homework or discipline of some kind, but otherwise I want to show them the brighter side of life; dare I say, so far it seems to be working. They are thriving, their spirits are light and fluffy. I don't know how they remain so seemingly unaffected by this tsunami in their lives, perhaps not for long?

As for me – I exercise when I can, I have three meals a day, I work possibly at half mast but with moments of inspiration. I call and speak to people about all this, write the odd heartfelt email which stops me ever committing anything else to paper. I have a 'to do' list as long as . . . which creates a low hum of stress in my life. My grasp on current affairs is zero, snippets from NPR radio as I buzz around in my protective hybrid tank from one mission to another. I 'push' things along.

I had a spree with your Heal cream, calling, emailing anyone I thought might be able to help us sell it, promote it, sanction it, endorse it! I copy out the science of it and in my bleary-eyed state try to commit it to memory. When people then ask me about it, I have the facts down. I'll never forget how much work you put into launching this idea. This 'range' that would mean perhaps one day you could give your nimble hands a rest and make money from your business enterprise. I remember you saying, 'Arthritis, a crushed finger and it's over – I can't work. I have to find another way to be productive alongside operating.'

The science of this skin gel . . .

What's the secret of Heal? Heal owes its effectiveness to ingredients that are soothing, help in repair and are anti-scarring.

The soothing group
Arnica montana: a plant-derived anti-inflammatory. This has been shown in clinical trials to significantly reduce bruising and swelling. When the smallest of your body's blood vessels are damaged, they let blood leak into the cells around, and as the haemoglobin in the seepage breaks down it discolours the skin – result, bruises.

Madecassoside: a valued and valuable plant-derived anti-inflammatory . . .

I have all the 'science' clipped into my diary . . .

There were legal problems with the website, so I have let our 'Heal drive' lull for a while. I shall now try to resurrect enthusiasm, get addresses of more people and gather some momentum again. I want to do anything I can for you, anything to extend you, celebrate you, keep you here for a little bit longer. Sometimes that just manifests in talking about you to potential business people, to Norman, to anyone who'll listen. You'd be happy to know that loads of donations have been made to FTW* in your memory. Sarah DJ is devoted – she'll never let FTW sink even though its captain is no longer at the helm. There's masses and masses of tributes written on FTW website about you, and kind words written to me and the boys. Sarah is printing, keeping copies of all of them for me to read when we're back. I'll put them in the boys' boxes with everything else – these boxes will be their 'time capsules' one day.

I think about our baby boy growing inside me – I'm incredibly excited to meet him. I will have a hot little body strewn across me to stroke, shell ears and a brand-new face to marvel at. I remember you saying holding a newborn was like 'passing around a soggy bag of chips'.

I'm overwhelmed at the prospect of trying to work creatively, support the four of us financially and give them the individual input they need. I'll do it – it's just I want to do it well and I know I'll hate myself if I fail. That's stupid; all parents fail. I must remind myself – that would happen even if you were here.

My alarm has gone off. I will end here and go to downtown LA to pretend we're in New York in 1994. It's a very good script this week, lots to hold on to. I love you, Monkey, so much, just love you, miss you, so desperate to feel you, hold you. I suddenly wish I'd done more of that, then I shut myself up. I did – you were everything to me. But I want to do it all over again and be better this time, less selfish, just give you everything I have.

All is well, you were so passionately loved by me – I wanted to spend my WHOLE life with you though.

Did you know, my love, you might not make it to the end? That's ridiculous and impossible. You are too important, too vital not to be a part of this any more, I cannot accept it. I love you so much it bursts out of me in huge heaving sobs sometimes.

I have all this love still left to give you. It's as if you have left too early on Christmas Day and half of your presents remain unopened.

* Facing the World (the charity Martin co-founded)

I am writing to your father to ask if we can visit him. I know you wanted this so I will make it happen. The boys will wreak havoc. I'm sure it will be the one day they behave terribly and you can laugh and not worry a bit from wherever you are!

You are in me. I hope I am still a part of you, my love, I carry you everywhere – I need to, I couldn't bear life otherwise.

Friday 11th July

Otis said today: 'I wonder why the gods wanted to take Dadu?'

I think all your input until now has given them this feeling of being incredibly loved. The most loved boys. We at least have you, different pieces of you, here, distributed amongst us.

Otis and I were having croissants later on today in 3 Square Café on Abbot Kinney. He was leaning his head against the rough white wall and he said something quite remarkable.

'I have two wishes, first is that I can make people come back alive again and the other is that I can control time and space, because then *I* could be in charge, not God.'

He's just turned five years old, where does it come from?

These boys, they jolt me into living, into embracing all that is still here. They are so inspiring, thank god, thank god we made them before you had to leave.

Later

I so miss feeling that 'wanted'. I hope and imagine wherever you are you are still wanting me. Do you know how much I'm wanting you? I couldn't miss you more, I didn't know missing could be this bad. In the past the missing you has been finite, what will bring it to an end this time, my own demise, dementia, death?

Will we be reunited in some strange way, do you think?

I don't care how – I don't even care if it's in a *Solaris* kind of a way. I want to talk to you, my love, ask you everything, know what happened to you, what was going on for those last moments. I can't bear the thought of you alone even though I know that's exactly how you would have wanted it to happen, given a choice.

I saw a severely disabled man the other day. A woman was feeding him in a sandwich bar. His hands were like two raw fat sausages placed on the slabs of his armrests. He could blow through a tube to steer the wheelchair. And that was it, his life shattered to smithereens. He could blow through a tube. Would that be any better? I struggle with that one. I often feel I want you back on any terms . . .

I just can't believe our world, our idyllic bubble, has been emptied of you. I can step back into it so easily though and feel you, smell you, see your smile that makes everything right. I want to keep that place for us; I want a place where I can visit you inside my head. I'm going to keep this huge space – I don't know where it will be kept as it's my heart, head, pieces of me that are yours. It doesn't matter – what makes me happy right now is that I can still find you; you haven't completely gone.

The boys and I went for a sunset walk along Abbot Kinney. We came across a band playing music that you'd love and there were two bass guitarists. One of them had a bright green bass guitar . . . Was that you shrieking to us?

Saturday 12th July

Only two weeks until I can go home and less than that for the boys. I think I want to go back so badly because it's *us* there in our house. Well, you're behind it now, buried. I want to turf you out and rescue your body, kiss it back to life.

I know I'll see you everywhere. I'm sure you'll rush up to me on the Fulham Road, bound up the stairs in our house and squeeze me or kiss me on the way.

I hope you are out there somewhere and know that I am still

here, all yours. As your wedding ring says: 'This is me encircling and embracing you for every minute of every day forever more.'

Would it have been better to know the length of our 'forever more'?

Oh god, I've just remembered a conversation with Norman.

'Tash, just a small thing . . . When I went to say goodbye to him, I saw his wedding ring and realised you'd probably want it. I've given it to Eve to give to you.'

I think I was silent for a moment.

'Oh, Norman, you are so lovely to think of that . . . It's just . . . it's strange . . . It has to stay on his finger. You see I had this inscription put on the inside before we got married. It said, "This is me . . ."'

I didn't make it much beyond that word. Fuck, now I've made him feel terrible.

'Tash, it's not a problem. I'm going to the morgue tomorrow to put it back on.'

And that was all that was said. He knew, he understood, however tenuous that link, it was a link, some idealised connection I might still have with you.

What incredible friends you had.

I just read the final script of the season. There's a line about a 'bastard baby' I just don't think I can say it. I attempted to leave Tom (the creator) a message about this and I just blubbed on his voicemail instead. I know he's going to feel terrible about it and that wasn't the point. I don't want to say it in the read-through or in the show as I know I'll crumble. It's not even pertinent to our situation. It triggered something though, inexplicable, a baby with no daddy? No, my baby with no daddy to meet him. I don't have any self-pity, not yet anyway. I can't have pity for my baby either, he's not born, I don't even know what he may or may not need. It's that, it's that there is no chance, no choice, no possibility of him meeting the man who made him. He can't track you down when he's ready, or if he should feel like it, he can't tell you to fuck off in a hate-filled adolescent fury, none of them can. That's important though, that's their right.

24th July

It's annoying because every time I sit down to write to you or about you, the heaving in my heart starts and tears flow and in public that's hard. I am so limited to where and when I can grab time to write about you. At least you put a baby in me before you left. I keep remembering that conversation we had in the hacienda in Mexico: should we dare to have another baby or was that just too crazy piling on yet more responsibility . . .?

What an amazing place we started our holiday in, all organised by you. Those last three holidays, the Christmas trip, skiing at Easter and you coming to visit us in LA before this hell, they were so special. I am glad we were always reckless, lived everything now, never held anything back for later.

I keep wondering when we can pick up again. When we can carry on our incredible journey and then I remember: you're gone from here, it's not possible, it's absurd! YOU of all people. You're so light, your touch is so deft and you always rather typically left everyone wanting more of you.

I have to sort out so many logistical things – financial – I must remortgage the house. Is that the advantage of death – no mundanity? Otis says, 'Dying is just like having the biggest sleeps of your life.'

I am on a plane to shoot the exteriors in New York. I feel these huge bursts of love escaping from me heading towards you, some-where, anywhere. You are with me, aren't you? I have to believe that in moments you are watching. I hope the boys feel that too.

I am meeting someone tomorrow, before we shoot, in an attempt to win an endorsement campaign. I know, I am selling our souls down the river. This one probably won't happen but perhaps I'll be on the road to getting something lucrative before it's all too late, then I don't need to be this worried about money.

It's getting dark outside, we're crossing a time zone – could I quickly cross into your place? As usual, I am sure I won't sleep much tonight, so that will put a nail in the coffin of 'campaign' possibilities.

If you were with me my love, I would, I would sleep and wake on top of you flipping about with joy like a mermaid.

I'm reduced without you. Not only have you gone but you've taken with you the best part of me.

I find when I write in diaries and even now writing to you I feel self-conscious because you are not here – when you were here, writing to you was unselfconscious, words and thoughts flowed. I start to think I have to try to emulate one of the Brontë sisters or something – have you taken my 'ease' with you too?

I don't know how life will be without you. I can't bear to look at that landscape with you missing from it. I have to concentrate on the detail instead, one small step in some purposeful direction.

My mission is to feel everything, avoid nothing that scares me and lead our boys to see all that is still possible, rather than all that is now lost.

I hate myself so much sometimes. I have to push that away too, write all the crap down, get rid of it, not let it fester.

Our baby is bouncing around as I write. I love it when he does that, something joyous and free going on inside no matter what I'm feeling further up inside my head and heart. His tumbles take me out of it – I'm doing this alone, I know you are half of him, but this feels utterly alone. I am a 'mummy-daddy'.

Sunday July 27th

I am flying into London – at last! I must have slept for a couple of hours as when I woke I saw your face there and that usually means I have been out for a while.

Your beautiful, kind face will get me through anything and everything.

I missed you in New York. I remember we'd vaguely said that we'd do a trip there together soon. You loved NY; I think it could just about house your energy.

The shoot didn't amount to very much in the end – just 'Hank' and 'Karen' wandering around the streets of NY to different locations – it was definitely your idea of fun. After shooting on Friday we all went to dinner at a restaurant called Waverly Place, which is a place I could imagine us curling up in a corner of, laughing, touching and talking, talking, talking. It wasn't like 'going out', I was sort of embedded into the group – it felt like a continuation of the shoot. I don't think I could have faced it otherwise.

I padded down to the spa on Saturday a.m. before hair and make-up and sat in the jacuzzi. I imagined you sitting opposite me with rose petals scattered all around us as if we were back in Mexico with our future stretched out before us, when there were only flimsy surmountable obstacles in our way – you talking about and persuading me to have another, our very last baby . . . and look at me now.

After shooting in Union Square on market day, buying bread and sunflowers, we wrapped early.

I then ran down a couple of blocks to David Von Ancken (director of this last episode) and he'd managed to get me a ticket for Liam Neeson's one-man show in the Beckett Festival. It was a trilogy, but I could only see the first part before racing to the airport. Afterwards, Liam, who I don't know, gave me a big bear hug and said how sorry he was. He was incredibly genuine. He said he couldn't imagine it – he has two boys; his expression was slightly tortured. Ralph Fiennes was there too, and said 'sorry for your trouble' which is such an Irish expression; it sounded different there coming from his lips. Everyone is so quiet and kind.

I felt like you today cramming in everything I possibly could and defying time. I even grabbed a drink with Susie before the matinee and she bought the boys a couple of beautiful shirts.

Friday 1st August

We're at the cottage, which I know will make your heart sing.

The boys have pegged downstairs to watch *Blake and Mortimer*, another 'you' influence. Zappy is curled up at the foot of our bed, looking annoyingly entitled to everything around her.

We have created something magical down here. I was thinking last night how much you had completed before you died. I wonder if I am able to keep this all going . . .

The electrics aren't functioning properly, so the fridge isn't working at the moment. In fact, nothing much is working. The same in London – BT, the internet, the television, it's all malfunctioning. I had a flicker, a moment wondering, *Is this how souls make their exit?* But I was snapped back to reality as I heard water hissing from the bathroom. You would have laughed so much, your wifelet standing there with an enormous bump and water jetting into her face and really not a CLUE what to do. I do know now, though, you see, so you can stop grinning. I've learnt something! Eve's Jacques showed me how to handle 'jet streams' . . . Perhaps I'll go on a plumbing course and pack in a mechanics course too. Don't you think there should be a course like that – just a week's crash course in how to be 'handy'?

I feel as if I am wasting days and days on the phone to BT or waiting in for electricians, plumbers and people from the gas company. Life has become an endless line of these secretive people with mysterious explanations; they can smell ignorance and accordingly zeros keep getting added to the bill. I know this would never happen if you were here.

I can hear the boys from here – their tinkling laughs. You used to say Theo's laugh was like a church bell pealing.

Otie said the other day: 'My two favourite things about Dadu are that he married you and that he had us.' I felt honoured!

I can't believe you are gone forever; this is fucking absurd. I have this insistent idea that you are peaceful. I would have imagined you to be SO frustrated at everything you haven't quite finished and everything you are missing. I know not being here for your boys must be agonising and not even meeting number three is nothing short of fucking ridiculous . . .

I've drifted now, staring out of the window into nature. Is that where the answers lie?

The electrician has arrived. My stomach is churning . . .

1 a.m. same night

I'm still unable to sleep most of the time. I should probably try now whilst there's still time. I miss you indescribably. I can't believe this is forever, you not being here. You are so much a part of me, of everything I could want out of life. Without you, it all seems inconceivable. You are the best and the most anyone could ever wish for. You belong here, you were born to live and live, what's happened? I keep thinking of your lips, you're mine, how mine you were, how you loved all of me. How is that even possible? But you did; I was truly loved by you. The most complete experience of my life was your love.

Saturday 2nd August

We've all woken late. I let the boys use the PlayStation you must have bought for them whilst we were in LA. My god Theo thinks you are a psychic king!

We went over to Mark and Amanda's last night for a bbq. It was their Patrick's 14th birthday – he had ten friends staying over. He and his friends entertained Theo and Otis for about four hours. They had an incredible time. We got back here at about 10.30 p.m. and they conked out. It was another of these beautiful signs – how much our number three is going to thrive having two older brothers. Thank god our little one will have them if he can't have you.

So much of life is contemplating how I am going to keep all this going, how I can make it work without you.

That stupid man (whom you never trusted) has needless to say not yet given my deposit back on the rental house in LA. He now wants to charge me for parts and cleaning extras – arghhh! I can't tell you how much effort and expense was put into the upkeep of that place. I know none of this is about how the house was left.

He even said when he came to check it, I quote, 'Wow, you've left it in even better shape than when you took it!' It's some strange control or mind game, exerting power over someone he sees as defenceless who might not notice. It's ugly and cruel and I'm shocked.

We just went to start the car to go and collect Roy from the train station and the battery's dead! I'm so stupid. I left the lights on in the rush to carry the boys to bed last night.

Oh god, how does everyone fit all this into their lives – cars, insurance, houses where everything malfunctions, the usual bills and then the other less usual demands to join this or help with that, finding novel ways to make money which leaves almost nothing left for the boys. I keep having flashbacks to Jarndyce and Jarndyce passages in *Bleak House*. I now understand the terror of law courts. We're the three little piggies and some huge fucking wolf is trying to blow our house down. I won't let it happen. I feel both protected by you and totally exposed by the loss of you.

Then there are WIRES . . . chargers for everything; nothing works without one. I keep these wires and leads crammed into an Aladdin's basket. They lie in wait to confuse me, coiled and viperous. I'm sure they all lead somewhere, somewhere good even. How will I ever find my way if I can't unravel them? I feel a grey dull ache in the pit of my stomach, a portentous feeling, a loathsome feeling, when faced with these normal things everyone else seems to understand and get through. Tell me, I must shake myself into action, find a solution to this inertia. This intimidation must be hormonal. Oh, Monkey, where are you?

Later the same day, 5 p.m.

Oh good, I feel different. It's bright sunlight. I'm sitting down finally. The boys are tearing about, weaving in and out of a sprinkler that you bought for them, shrieking with delight.

I want to start responding to all the incredible letters we've received about you. I love reading other people's versions of you, craning my neck, poring over every word to see if there might be yet another revelation about you. I might get to know you even more deeply in death. I am so proud of you. I feel so lucky to have been a part of your magnificent life.

Late night

I'm lying thinking, yes, I can and will thrive again – I get that far. I imagine life without you.

I can't relate or fully hear anyone else right now apart from you. All my interactions are phoney, convincing to a point. Now I realise how we separated ourselves, us and maybe the boys too – I can relate to them but no one else yet.

I'm bumbling along, realising I can't really do anything practical. I have no idea how to work your computer. It leaves me stymied. Whilst my hopelessness is exposed I have to confess everything . . . BT internet connection, Sky TV, music/sonos programme which is also embedded in your computer . . . it all feels so mysterious and inexplicable. I reach for various handbooks and feel immediately nauseous as I open them. I know a film, a thick fog, will descend somewhere between me and the page. My glaring incompetence – arghhhh, I am pathetic!

I don't want to hear music right now. It makes me crumble – all the notes are so wrapped up in you – but perhaps I shouldn't be so selfish. I'm sure the boys would like to whirl to the thump and beat of something loud, some 'Back in Black' perhaps . . .?

'Blackbird', that song you so desperately wanted me to sing at your 40th, and I couldn't, I just couldn't do that for you. I would do it now, I would do ANYTHING for you now. I shan't be able to listen to that for a long time.

Everything's throbbing, not only my eyes. Veins are popping out everywhere. The support tights help but I can't believe I've ten more weeks of this. It's ridiculous but it's difficult to do anything physical, stand for any period of time, walk, run errands, etc. It's a foretaste of old age. I feel disabled. It will be hard to be permanently reduced to this one day. I am just thinking how much you would loathe being incapacitated like this, thinking how it's good after all that you didn't 'half go', thinking yes, you died at the summit, you had the best of everything, your potential was realised.

Monday 4th August

I woke up dreaming of you at about 4 a.m. Sometimes I can still feel you, just about, but all this is fading. How can it after only a few months? Perhaps I'm pushing all these sensations away? I don't have time to live in this realm with you, this dreamlike state I keep sacrificing sleep to be in. In our real life we had that – tumbling about, literally fooling around as if we had all the time in the world. You MADE time, you manipulated it, stretched it out of shape to suit our purposes; you never made anything between us feel rushed. We lay in baths to talk, rolled around laughing on our bed, talking always of our future; none of the mundanity of life seemed to seep through. Now life is only this trudge, this endless list of tasks, these 'to do' lists that afford me a moment's reprieve once I've written them only to realise seconds later I don't know how 'to do' half the things on them! I KNOW I should learn how to change a tyre, but really honestly I just don't fucking want to . . .

Oh dear, you married an incompetent!

I am finding some solace in the fact that no one seems able to crack through your vastly complicated computer system.

I'm going to find a 'geek'. I remember you always predicting that geeks would one day rule the world. Well, my darling, they ARE about to rule my world . . .

I feel embarrassed at seeming so lacking in independence. Somehow you can be independent by being interdependent with someone else. We were perfect for each other in that way: we shaded in the colours the other person couldn't or didn't want to.

You made my universe so much of what it was. You were this globe beaming light, pulsating energy.

Monday 11th August

It's very early, 4 a.m. again, dark. I woke with thoughts of you – what else? I tried to remember all the ways you touched me and live in hope I will be able to copy you. You were an amazing lover. I want one of your 'squeeze the life out of me' hugs where I'm in danger of being crushed or consumed by you.

How could this happen? Where are you?

I feel as if I am a big bear lost in a cave with no entrance or exit. Can humans understand death?

Your tiniest boy kicks life back into me. It's a fantastic feeling juxtaposed to the desperate, howling emptiness left behind by you.

I've been raw and devastated about you for the last few days, unable to stem my sobs – weirdly, always when the boys are sleeping or out. There is a dam breaking – I'm doing my best with all this grief – it doesn't have to be so bad. When I think of you, even though it tears my heart out, it brings a kind of tranquillity too. You are my home, my port, my place. I love you, all of you, all over again and again. I won't bore either of us with the logistical, financial, practical trauma sweeping over our lives; I can't bear to give it more time and space than it's already inhaling. I will find a way to make everything work.

This is challenging every weakness I have – every button I hate being pushed is being pushed, I am totally exposed and incompetent! I must go before the kids wake up. I need to gather ammunition and intelligence for the solicitors this morning. Pray, my Monkey, this all turns out right.

Tues 12th August

Have been gathering all info for solicitors, conversations with banks, history stretching back eight years ago to when we bought our house. There was some case in the press about a mother who had lost her husband. He hadn't left a will – they were young – and it now fell upon the widow to sue her children in order to keep her house. There was some legal loophole that left this as the only option for her not to lose everything in trust to them until they were eighteen. (They are a baby and toddler now.) The first solicitor I had suggested that this could be one of my options along with other fairly bleak options which go against everything we had tried to plan. I have been so stressed by this side of things since you died. I don't want to write about it as this is my time/space for switching an 'off' button on all of that and reaching out to you instead.

The good news is Robert Craig (new solicitor) has a road we can now travel down with far less complication . . . Let's see. He inspires absolute faith in me and is very human – he even loves the theatre!

There is endless other time-consuming crap. Have to write a letter to BT, no other way to get a phone to work . . .

Here's my notes below, let me amuse or bore you up in your heaven . . .

8/8/08 main phone line not working.

Technician had come previous Fri 1/8/08 and reported the line was perfect.

We could not get internet access either – they accidently took the broadband off – mixed messages. 'But you will have to speak to a separate dept about all of that . . .'

I had already settled a large bill for calls & engineer call-outs £478.77 over the phone the week before on 28/7/08 visa card.

*A page of notes re all calls & times made to BT on 8th & 9th August
– a total of 11 hours spent waiting/holding/explaining whilst our
little boys bounce off the walls . . .*

*Tried to arrange another appoint. for engineer to come & chk
exchange, fix our phone. BT said they would call me straight back
with an appoint., call not returned.*

*Finally 'their system went down' on Sat 9th – so we were unable to
book a time for an engineer to come – arghhhhh!*

*They said they would call me at 10.15 on Sunday, which they did, to
arrange an appoint for Monday (ha – making progress . . .)*

*Engineer due to arrive between 8 a.m.–1 p.m. on Monday 11th
August (I'm now in London w boys to meet solicitors) so Tony was
waiting for the BT man to call him. They had all his contact details
and mine and did not call or show up.*

*I am now in a queue attempting to reach Vishal Vidya who I made the
appoint. with on the phone. I have his pin, oh yes I do – 2923!*

*He assured me I would be able to reach him through this no. very
quickly and that the engineer would arrive without fail at the
cottage today.*

*So far have been waiting listening to 'your call is important to us . . .'.
Oh, but no it fucking isn't – who recorded that? They're putting on
a soft sort of psychiatrist's voice, all concerned. How can you
sound so earnest, so genuine, and not mean it?! For 43 mins I have
now been 'held in a queue'. I'm not being 'held' – BT, you have no
rights to use those words. You must change that recording to 'You
are now being dropped, dumped in a queue and we really couldn't
give a shit what happens next . . .'*

*8.46 p.m. I spoke to Santosh finally who was unable to give me his
surname. The phone went dead. I wanted to cry, but I shall NOT
because I am a grown woman. Oh fuck, come on, Natascha, none
of this matters, just laugh, you MUST laugh.*

*I try again. I ask for Vishal as he was so understanding when we last
spoke (even if he did later betray me). I forgive him now, let's put it
all behind us – to err is human – let's move forward and book a*

*definitive appointment. Please, Vishal, answer your extension, I
love you, you're the only one who understands the interminable
saga, I can't, I just can't start all over again!*

This is what happened with the man before Vishal:
*I said by way of explanation: 'I think this has happened because I had
to change the name on the account . . . No, you can't speak to the
original account holder, but I am his wife . . . No, it's not possible,
you see, he has actually, actually he's died.'*
*'I am so sorry, madam, for your loss. We will have to close the account
down and open a new account in your name. You might be able to
retain this phone number. I will just check.'*
*YOU ARE FUCKING KIDDING ME! (I didn't say that – I exhaled
loudly.)*
*Keep calm, otherwise they'll hang up. Oh god, there's nothing I can
do – again, even in this mundane situation, as with the colossal
one, I am utterly powerless! Is that why this urge to cry keeps rising
back up? Where did I ever get the impression I had a handle on
things . . .?*
*I am not allowed to speak to Vishal, even though that is his pin – he
should not have given it to me because the phone exchange is too
large.*
*Another Santosh said that, yes, someone had been booked to come
and check out the phone line. He did not know what had gone
wrong but would call me back on my London no. where I am now at
9.10 p.m. on 11/8/08.*

*It's 9.50 p.m. – we have an appointment between 1 p.m.–6 p.m.
Friday 15th August to resolve the broadband problem.*

That will be seventeen days of life on and off trying to resolve
a tiny problem. Angel, what will happen if there's a big serious
fucking problem? How will I ever juggle all this? And also how is
it that everything, I mean 90% of things, in our house are malfunctioning? What, *what*, is going on?

I must sort everything out before the baby comes, just can't be drowning in this, I need all my energy for these cubs.

Another day in August

I have just switched on my computer and found emails I sent to your mother – is it awful to include her like this when she is struggling so much with her own grief? Or is it right, she won't be a lone ship in the night if I keep flashing my own dying torch her way?

28th August

I am very tired. I hate to admit this, but it is the truth. I don't feel I have enough time to think about you or what's happened – no time to cry even; it's too much of an imposition. There's too much that needs to be done before that. I know how deeply frustrated you would be if you could see all this mess and you were so careful compared to me. I would have left you in a far worse state. I'm trying to sort all that out now. I think I might be nearing a solution, finding someone to rent or timeshare on the cottage. Simon Binder is helping – he's so selfless; people are amazing.

I'm going into the hospital for a quick growth scan now. It makes my eyes well up every time I go into that place, that place where you worked so hard, where your boys were born and then where you were pronounced dead . . .

Later

Everything was good on the scan; all the measurements were in the right place, etc.

I'm back at home after getting the boys. They are both extremely tired and stroppy. I've come upstairs for a breather.

I miss you so so much and just can't let any of this show in front of them. I must remain like a rock they can crash against and I will be that, but I do need my moments with you, my thoughts of you, these memories. I'm still using you as a source of wisdom and guidance. Baby, I just can't believe that you've gone, that you're not coming back. I think I only SEEM fully functioning because I carry you around or the love and comfort I got from you still floats about me. The idea that you've gone is just too unbearable, too absurd, too impossible. You are my gorgeous man, that figure of incredible vitality and vigour, of endless energy.

Tuesday 9th September

Oh baby I'm losing you. I'm getting used to this life of an automaton. There is nothing in between the tasks, the endless lists, the knowledge that there will be more lists, that things will continue to break, malfunction and need fixing again and again, and for some reason there seems to be an overwhelming amount of that and very little resolution of it. Where are you? Where is the fun? Where is the reward, the hug, the kiss, that big warm shadow of you falling across me as you enter the room?

Are you slipping because this is the longest period in our lives that we would have been apart? Will you come back? I mean the feeling of you – will that come back and surround me again? Are you around the children, can they feel you or is this it? No time for you to put a full stop on your life, to hug and press against us, to leave an imprint, to tattoo us with you.

I suppose your DNA has done that for you. You will be around forever, your likeness will infect us – scattered, treasured particles of you can be found in others. I am grateful for that, but I want you, my love. You are ebbing away so quickly . . . our baby is not even here yet. Is that why, am I making room for him?

I'll be surrounded by people where I pretend, people who don't care at all – why should they? They are paid to help; it's just a job. By this I mean useful, essential help – cleaner, babysitter, accountant, solicitor – all practical helpers, but there's this line in red right across the page, as it should be: a professional transaction. I probably had an imbalance of love and passion fed to me before, that's why all this mundanity seems so bold and unbearably bright now. You smothered it before, coloured in all that was grey; there was no space for that with you. Somehow it all got done whilst you were dreaming music, puzzles, rhythms, jokes and adventures in your head.

I don't know where the boys' heads are about you. I can't push them. I want to open a little trapdoor into their brains and see how it's all functioning. Can I explain anything better, piece any of it together for them? The evenings are crowded and stressed with obligations, having to reprimand them in order to get them to do anything. I hate being like this, inventing endless rules that they need to abide by and then promising a reward for the tiniest task. I want to leave all this space for their thoughts, feelings – anything they want to share. Instead this bureaucracy is crashing through, rough, aggressive waves of it churning me about. I want to be lolling and lying with you on an imaginary seabed somewhere, smiling bubbles.

One of your patients is trying to 'retrospectively sue' you, well, *sue me* now. Apparently, no complaints before you died. I don't know the details yet – other than she has now approached the practice, dissatisfied with her result.

The guys said it will be dealt with by the MDU.

Saturday 13th September

My angel, it's only a month until your third little boy is due to arrive on this earth.

I can and will bear anything from here on. The throbbing of missing you drums on. I found a beautiful birthday card from you, in fact it dropped out of this diary yesterday. I think it was your writing and feelings for me which choked me. I feel blessed to have been loved by you – you gave me the best life, the best love, the most heavenly pups.

Saturday 20th September

I'm sorry I can never find a second to write except in the wee small hours. I'm sitting up in bed. We arrived down in the cottage last night (I have found people to rent for three weekends a month; it will be a lifesaver . . .)

I'm staring at your shirts hanging on the back of the door. Hanging there, stupid and hopeless with no owner, apologising to me.

I had a very good sob yesterday after dropping the boys off at school. I had the house to myself, so I dared to take an infusion of you and felt the loss deeply and achingly. I was in your office attempting to be efficient, printing documents out and bam it hit me all over again.

Oh fuck I love you so much, so so much. Every time I look at this birthday card and read it, I feel like the most loved woman on the planet. I look at the picture I have of you on my screen saver and I just want to eat you off it. It looks possible. Pictures on computers are more lifelike; there's a 3D-ish element to them. I want to join you, peel back the plastic and crawl under it to lie next to you. Is that where you might be hiding, in my computer?

I don't know if I understand what's happened. I think I do and then I suddenly don't, sitting here alone in your dream cottage that we lovingly devised together. Oh you would be so happy here right now. Your boys are cuddled up tight in front of hard-earned Saturday morning TV. It's toasty warm thanks to all the work that was done and there's a huge fog hanging over the valley and bird-song trying to break through.

I had better go and 'breakfast' these chimps before they get hypo. I miss you searingly, constantly, and want every bit of you back. As Otie said last week, 'I want Dadu back alive, now!'

It would have cut you in two – your little boy loves you so much.

Sunday 5th October

I'm listening to your favourite radio station, FIP. I had a terrible missing-you moment this morning. I was talking to Neil on the phone and he asked me about my 'birth plan', which of course I don't have other than to imagine you, to summon you up with all my might. I reminisced to him about the last time, when Otie was born.

Do you remember running up and down the stairs between me and your operating theatre? Finally he had the courtesy to come at about 7.30 in the evening when you had finished your day's work. The sun was setting outside the window, I fainted after pushing him out and I woke up to see you and Mark upside down each one of you gripping an ankle so the blood would rush to my head. It all felt perfectly normal at the time – how undignified it must have been thinking back. And where was the baby? I didn't believe you when you said another boy.

'Oh, he's over here,' said Mark. 'He's not the one who needed attention!' And he scooped him up and brought him over to me. Where's the ginger hair from? He was my little Irish pug! You then ran out to Ed's Diner to get burgers and chips and a bottle of champagne and we had the most beautiful 'post birth' time together with me feeding him and you feeding me.

As I was describing the scene to Neil I felt full of joy and he was laughing, then in a flash as I reached the end of the description, I dissolved into sobs. They rose up from my belly like irrepressible bubbles. He was silent. I don't know if he was crying too.

I know this is quite out of character, but I'm making a Sunday roast for the boys. The Aga is playing up so I'd better check it's not all burnt to a crisp – be back soon if I don't get intercepted on the way.

I wonder if by writing to you so much – I know it's mundane and boring but that is the point with birth and death – the most transformative experiences in our lifetime and yet they both demand such a practical response. It is necessary to chart each stage after this apocalypse – by writing to you so much, does it mean I keep my sanity? It's my pretence at still being with you, still being in a relationship; yes, the ultimate in long-distance relationships.

I have been fine the last two days, as long as I'm being productive and crunching through things and as long as I can keep you in my midst. I gaze at the photo I have of you on my screen saver. Fuck, I love you so much! This is only the beginning without you, just the beginning. There are so many conversations I want to have with you, so many more things I want to share with you, so many more adventures we haven't yet been on, not least the one brewing in my tummy. Who is he? Who will he become? Will he have you coursing through his veins even though you are no longer here?

I am incredibly excited to meet him despite all the chaos and craziness of these circumstances. The boys and I made a plan yesterday of who would be in charge of what. Otie has elected to be in charge of burping him and is riveted by the idea of the odd fart popping out as a bonus and Theo has nominated himself as his 'entertainer' and would like to carry him around in a Baby Bjorn sling. We have become a tight team.

I have terrible imaginings of the kids and roads. I know you did too. I think it was one of the things that drove you to shout at them – your fear of losing them, traffic, hot water, fire – how to teach danger without throttling their appetite for adventure?

We were in the car the other day and Theo started to recount a road-rage incident of yours. It was such a long time ago but he remembered it vividly. I tried to explain that it was prompted by a strong protective paternal instinct. (Am I covering for you too much? Should I pull you down off the pedestal and criticise you a bit here and there? Oh god, I can't just yet . . .) I explained you were trying to defend us against the recklessness of other people on the road. We laughed – they would much rather hear stories of their Dadu – the rebel, the iconoclast, than the good doctor hero.

After recounting the incident, Theo asked me if there were any other times when you had lost your temper like that. I told them we used to live in Paris and I became pregnant with him there. You were so proud and excited about your heavily pregnant wife. One night on the way home from a jazz club we were crossing a zebra crossing and a guy on his moped decided to show off and speed up as he approached the zebra crossing, expecting to scare us and see us run to the other side. Instead (I can see their faces in the rear-view mirror at this point, mouths agape at this Parisian's audacity) you chased the moped and yanked the guy off his bike as it careened into the island in the middle of the road. They laughed hard, loving the idea of you leaving him stranded to chase after his bike.

Thursday 9th October

Baby, I have nothing to say. This has been the strangest and most normal few months. I am bringing the baby to the forefront of my mind. I can't think of you so consistently. Nature has barged in and is forcing this pressing, exciting new life into your place. I am gathering energy from it and feeling very positive about it. The boys spoke about you more than usual today. It was hard for me to rein in my feelings and not cry, but I managed it. I want to write more about this when I'm not so tired. They said some wonderful things and wrote and drew pictures of you. You would be spectacularly proud of them right now, they are two very special little people. I am thinking so much of our next little boy.

We will no longer have someone missing – we shall be a burgeoning flourishing foursome again.

No date. Loose pages from my diary

I don't think I wrote about the trip to the twenty-week scan. The one I had originally booked in LA for us to go to together when you came back out. When I was back arranging your funeral, I dashed into the hospital to talk to Mark. He went through ALL the options with me. He is such an amazing man. Can you imagine if I'd elected not to have the baby, or if the shock . . . if that flattish stomach I woke up with the morning after you died had meant something more portentous than it did. His time is so precious and yet we talked for a while and in the end he said: 'This baby will be such a blessing to you.'

I asked him if he'd ever had a patient whose husband had died whilst she was pregnant. He looked at me very directly and said, 'No, I haven't.' After a pause, he said, 'I have had patients who were left though, who separated.'

I somehow thought that might be even worse, at least I was always wanted by you.

I cried a great deal in that consultation. I was having to confront the future and somehow he was helping me to do it. This man who had delivered our last baby into your hands was going to deliver this one too. That's as close as I can get.

He was sure everything was fine. However, he said to go to a place on Harley Street to get my twenty-week scan done very thoroughly. He used his contacts and got us in to see a consultant the next day I think.

I had perhaps misguidedly thought it would be fun for the boys to come and watch their baby sibling bobbing about in amniotic fluid. I asked your mum if she'd like to come too and she did, boldest and bravest mama she is. It was tough. Theo was exhausted from a sleepover the night before, a 'wakeover', and didn't feel great. Otie wanted to squirt the jelly all over the eminent consultant and he did . . .

Unlike the three-month scan you actually can't see as much. It's all in close-up and you don't see the whole body, so I think it was hard for the boys to grasp. When his heart came up and they could see the chamber and the little 'hammer' knocking away at a frantic pace, the boys wanted that to be checked. 'Will it always knock that fast?' They don't miss a trick. I wonder if hearts will always have a double meaning for them?

Anyway, he told us it was a boy, which they were both thrilled about, particularly Otie. He had firmly predicted it was a boy right from when we told him I was pregnant in the Urth Caffé on your last trip to LA. I am SO glad we told them together – thank god we didn't delay it. I remember going to the farmers' market all together and you picking out some baby clothes, very unlike you – but you bought a black T-shirt with a sort of rubbery pink rose stuck on to it, probably more 'Guns N Roses' than 'girl'. You said, 'This is on the remote off-chance we have a girl . . . but I know it's a boy. We're going to have three boys – I can't wait!'

Your baby clothes are waiting to be tried on, neatly folded at the top of my 'hospital bag'. I thought fleetingly about taking your favourite old shirt to wrap him in – it still smells of you – but then that suddenly seemed morbid.

Friday 10th October

I was just walking along Jermyn Street. I saw trilbies and beautiful men's shirts in shop windows. I instinctively moved towards the door of the shop before reality kicked in and cancelled the impulse to rush in and buy you something. There is no 'man to love', to treat and buy things for. I used to love doing that, being able to make you smile in another way, not because of the 'bought thing' but your realising that I think of you so much throughout the day.

I am the size of a large semi-detached house and I cannot ever imagine not being. I now know how obese people feel. It must be dreadful – constantly breathless, vascular problems, lower back aches, unable to run or even sit comfortably and an insatiable desire for more food.

I want to sleep for a long time.

Something or someone is looking after me as I had another voice-over today. I think I have one on Monday too, which may end up being lucrative. Our house is also being booked for the odd photo shoot so there is a little money rolling in from that. I'm just thinking about how much you would hate that: people, strangers, being in our house, amongst our things, amidst our private life, leaving their trash and smells behind. There is no choice, which makes every decision SO much easier. We definitely had too much choice before.

By the way, the GlaxoSmithKlein meeting went well this morning. You would have felt proud of your Heal thus far.

My brain is mush. I've been trying to learn the names of the active ingredients that underpin this brilliant invention since last May.

'Arnica montana, madecassoside, haloxyl,' and so on, then I stumble and forget the names of the others – 'that's the "soothing group" . . . well, some of the ingredients,' I haltingly say. Then I move swiftly on to talk about the 'repair group' and the 'anti-scarring' group, hoping no one notices how quickly I hop off the slippery unfamiliar terrain of scientific words. It's like learning another language. You learn one expression perfectly with a good accent and clutch on to it until the native speaker smiles and fires a whole artillery round of words back at you, and shamefully you have to come clean: '*No hablo . . . er . . . Español.*' It is thus with my ignorance of anything scientific . . . Theo will explain everything to me in a year or two.

I remember Ant used to say, 'Most people "name drop" but Martin just "organ drops".'

I have to stick to the basics otherwise I'll end up underselling it instead of helping it to become the rip-roaring success it should be. If only we had a more cohesive infrastructure, a good managing director, I know we would get a fantastic deal and this would be a household product. Everyone would have a little pot in their medicine cupboard. Didn't tell you but gathered some lovely quotes in June from actresses and others, who did a trial with it. It has had an enormous amount of publicity, well, by my reckoning. It's now about getting the distribution right, that's what is not working – that and the website. You would fix all this with a magic wand like a wizard . . .

The point is I won't let it fade away (and neither will Norman and the others, by the way. My god, that man is tenacious!). Forget what you and they have invested in it – it's the 'you' in this little pot I can't give up on.

Kelly Cole dropped by the house when we were still in LA. I showed him the little reel of footage of you. He was desperate to see it because he couldn't make it over to London for your wake. Anyway, he wanted to help with getting things back on track. I showed him the Heal Gel and the literature and he was inspired to take it around all the fashion PR people he knows. I had put it all in a kind of Jiffy bag, which he'd laid on the sideboard as we finished talking. We started our goodbyes and Theo suddenly thrust the bag back into his hand and said:

'You musn't forget this, the Heal, Dadu invented it.'

There's something about that sentence that still catches in my throat. As oblivious as kids sometimes seem – playing with Lego on the floor or chiselling bits of paint off a doorframe – he got it; we needed to move this thing along. This legacy of yours couldn't be left to die as well.

After the meeting I made a list of what John from GSK wants info on. I have passed it on to Norman and Simon. They will now go to their head offices and see what might happen next . . . In turn John will explain what GSK can bring to the table.

Friday 10th October contd.

I miss your face so much, I miss your hard all-consuming embraces. I miss all the love you gave me and I miss not having you to give love to. Where's my co-pilot, my adventurer, my navigator?

Caroline Muir came over a while ago laden with an enormous delicious 'bake' of some kind. Unfathomable really . . . the sort of thing, well, for me it would be a feat akin to an asthmatic climbing Everest. She brought these sketch pads/writing diaries. They were sort of 'bespoke' for grieving children. At first, I shrank from them, they seemed a bit persuasive and heavy to me. I put them on the bookshelf and if the boys came across them they could make of them what they would.

This was all about six weeks ago. Anyway, last night they did uncover them and it was fascinating – well, it turned into an out-pouring really.

They both took the books into their beds and started sketching you and doing drawings of their feelings and what they looked like. They answered questions, listing your most prevalent characteristics, listing the cleverest thing you had ever done, the silliest, what they missed most about you and what they disliked. It was quite a revelation. It ended up being another outlet for their experiences and feelings at the moment, a record too for them later on. They may never complete them, toss them aside, get bored of them, but I'll add them to their memory boxes, finished or not. I want them to have their own record, not my version of all this. I am so grateful to Caroline, incredibly smart and generous of her.

She also so generously (along with lovely other people) offered to be my birthing something – can't remember the word. I can't imagine anything stranger than a girlfriend being down at the far end waiting for our baby to come out. I think I'm too private for that. Either *you're* there and if you're not, well then it's just me and my 'projected you' floating around me, giving me courage, making me smile, giving me all the strength I need. If you can't be there, there's no replacement for you, so there's no point pretending there is. I will be alone, but not for long. This new life will be arriving, whatever the circumstances – that's a miracle, perhaps even more so.

Saturday 11th October

My love, I feel inconsolably sad right now. I am sitting by your graveside, doing some fairly full-on unencumbered grieving. I can't believe your body or I suppose what's left of it is still here buried underneath me. I so want it back, I want to pull you out of the ground to squeeze and hold you even if there are only pieces of you. I would brush all the dirt and insects off you and kiss you and hold you. Today, this minute, as I try to focus on these blurry words, I feel I cannot bear life without you. You mean so much to me. So much joy has been sucked away. In this minute a carcass of life, an imitation, shrouds me. Without you . . . god, I don't know. I don't understand.

Somehow you managed to stop me from being all the things I didn't want to be, for thinking thoughts I don't want to think. Your ripples are fading, a bright rainbow being reabsorbed into the dullness of an English sky.

As Beanie said at your graveside when we buried you: 'He was the best of men.'

There is no other you, no one even remotely close to you. I do wish you had a brother similar to you – so ironic that everyone in your life was so completely different from you and from one another.

You would love today. It is brilliant sunshine and there are red and gold leaves nestling up to me. Your grave looks proud and spectacular like you. It is surrounded by ancient stones from Fanad beach, which Noni and Roy lovingly hauled back from Ireland for you and me.

Tuesday 14th October

Your life policy came through today . . .

I have exhaled, but I daren't completely as I still feel anything could still go wrong somehow. The weight is lighter, though, thank you, thank you.

I have a notebook in which I scribbled down all my 'to do' lists a month or so after you died. I'm glad this part of losing you is at least now over and we are saved, safe for the moment, our life allowed to continue on. I feel so bloody lucky that you organised a life policy – how easily you could have overlooked that?

And, thank god, I have work to come. Work is SO underestimated – where would I be without it?

Wednesday 15th October

Angel, I've come into hospital to be induced as Mark is leaving for holiday. His sound advice is not to wait. I thought our baby might make an appearance the day before yesterday but he got shy. So I went for a very vigorous walk in the cemetery after dropping the boys. Today is the day and Damon's birthday too!

I'm in the very early stages, waters have broken, no induction yet – hurrah, might avoid that horrible drug – he's giving me a few hours on my own to get things moving.

I am contracting, but not painfully yet.

I cried, a quick, hard sob when I arrived in the hospital room. Pulled it in, can't spend the whole of labour grieving; this is going to be a celebration.

I started to play music and 'Blackbird' came up, hmmm, big mistake, still can't take music, particularly your favourite – fuck, beginning to rise and fall. I've decided we're closest to water as an element; inside me is the tenacious, relentless ebb and flow and it won't let me go until he is out.

I'm with him now, you have receded for the moment, I'm willing this little soul to come out. I'm dying to meet him and hold him in my arms, give him big kisses from you wherever you are. I know you are with me, angel, around me, in me. Even though you're dead, these genes, these cells of yours are multiplying, furiously doubling, tripling themselves, without you here to oversee, isn't that mad and wonderful? You are still growing – you have flouted all the rules, oh how I love you for that!

Things are becoming stronger ... I'll sign off for a minute, I love you for everything.

PART TWO

Thursday 16th October

He's here and perfect.

'. . . the tender soles of the feet that had come to us without touching the ground . . .'

Remember that other quote from *Earthly Paradise*? I'm ruining it but it was her marvelling at this new person who had arrived in the room without ever having crossed the threshold.

I am so sorry you're missing this. Our little boy is utterly divine. He's incredibly serious at the moment, brave, fiercely intelligent like you. He looks like a little squashed grape. I'm willing him to look like you – there isn't a whole lot of chin going on, though.

I didn't have to do the whole induction hell. Mark did break my waters and I progressed pretty well. He checked to see how much I had dilated about four hours later and apparently I hadn't very much. But after that examination the contractions got stronger and stronger and rocketed out of control – they completely over-whelmed me! My body went into shock and started convulsing and shaking. Oh dear, I felt utterly dreadful – nauseous, sweaty – my body became something I needed to exit from. Even though I was very quickly fully dilated within a few minutes, I couldn't maintain a still enough position to be able to push. I was a fish on a slab, flipping about purposelessly. I begged and hollered for an epidural. Mark was reluctant as he said I was already at the pushing stage. Even if I could bear the agony I couldn't keep my body still enough to push, I couldn't gather my force – my body wouldn't or couldn't listen to my brain; they had departed from one another and I was lost somewhere in the middle.

Whoever invented the epidural is a saint and genius. Even a

small dose at the 11th hour is nirvana. Oh my god what peace, what an elixir! My body and brain plugged into one another again and I rode the contractions like an expert surfer tunnelling waves. The contractions were no longer slamming into one another like wrecked cars. There was a moment of respite, some air in between each one. The other had been like a fairground ride that had spun off its own axis. I felt as if I was going to Mars with no breathing apparatus. Little one is wailing . . . will be back.

Friday 17th October

Remember that Sylvia Plath poem I read you after Otis was born (I think)? I read it to you in the car to entertain you whilst you were driving. I used to love reading you extracts of things you might love and always got very disappointed if my instincts were off and you didn't respond enthusiastically! This is so perfect, only a few pieces of it floating around though:

> Love set you going like a fat gold watch.
> The midwife slapped your footsoles, and your bald cry
> Took its place among the elements.
>
> . . .
>
> All night your moth-breath
> Flickers . . .
>
> One cry, and I stumble from bed, cow-heavy and floral
> In my Victorian nightgown.
> Your mouth opens clean as a cat's . . .
>
> . . . And now you try
> Your handful of notes;
> The clear vowels rise like balloons.

Our little boy is lying on the bed like a pod. Ridiculously perfect – you must be experiencing this somehow.

Of course I will project endlessly, but his eyes don't look like they are from my side – as the boys said with slightly shocked expressions when they met him: 'I wonder why he looks so Chinese?' I'm thinking of that beautiful lithograph Andy gave us as a wedding present – the one of the noble-looking Japanese boxer that I thought looked like you. Every time I walked past it in the hallway of my parent's flat it reminded me of you before I really knew you. You were somehow unreachable at that time, thank god for that, for me staying away from you – had I got too close we would have crushed what we have back then.

Anyway, he has that about him. All I can see is strength emanating from him. He's a gift.

I have some big decisions to make over the next week with work and how to earn the next instalment of money. I don't actually know what you would think, but I suppose we always tended to talk this stuff through and come to the same conclusion. I think overall for me to make money has become more important than it has been before and the only way to make it unimportant is to make some . . .

Yesterday and the night before I will treasure forever. I switched my phone off. I didn't tell anyone where I was apart from the kids thinking I had gone out for the night. Ania brought them to meet him in the morning – they had to be the first – and then they carried on to school. I had our baby boy as we would have done and stared at him for thirty-six hours. He's feeding pretty well when he does. He has huge sleepathons in between which I know won't last for long, but it's a lovely way for his life to start, easing us both in.

Tuesday 21st October (day 6 of baby boy 3's life)

I have held all my missing you inside of me for days now because I can't afford for it to explode out of me. The boys have just been collected by a Cameron House mother and taken to the park, and Baby is sleeping after feeding for most of the night. I can't believe I'm saying this, but I think I had forgotten just how exhausting the sleeplessness is. He woke every hour and a half to eat – the upside of which was my boobs didn't throb with the over-production of milk quite so much; the downside was obviously that I didn't get to sleep.

I just came upstairs to our room for a nap while all is quiet and thought, *I can let some of this feeling hang out, finally, just a tiny bit.* My practical side thought, *No, don't, you haven't got the time, grab half an hour's sleep instead.* I lay my head down obediently and your face flooded into my mind and that was it, the floodgates opened. I can't bear doing all this without you.

I was thinking even the people we know seem paler and less interesting without you around. I find I can't be with anyone, I am a flimsy echo with nothing to offer. I think you've extracted my juiciness and taken it with you. God oh god I wish you could come back. I can't keep this wishing and welling down any more. It's overflowing today. Hormones was day four but today it's you.

This disbelief I have: you can't be gone.

It was a challenge before, that idea, that practicality – could I do life without you? Yes is of course the answer. But the missing you, the wishing for your return, the intensity, is another fresh layer that's emerged with a new strength and ferocity. It's a bit like labour – I can cope with the waves of pain as they subside, the same with grief and losing you – but this – I would love an emotional epidural just for an hour to breathe without it turning into a sob. You just are the best person there ever was. All I want is to have you back.

This seems so impossible, that you YOU are over, finished, how could that happen? SOMEONE PLEASE MAKE THIS UNTRUE. Can I ask for one thing, can I even beg 'please, universe, bring him back'? I promise I won't tell anyone, we'll keep your re-emergence a secret. If this could be allowed just once, we would be sworn to secrecy, to never betray those sacred laws of life and death . . . just this once . . . It wouldn't alter any balance if no one ever knew about it, just us and the boys, and then you could meet him, your new one. You could touch his head, stroke his cheek, tell him you love him, show him where he came from.

> *You have taken the east from me; you have taken the west from me;*
> *You have taken what is before me and what is behind me;*
> *You have taken the moon, you have taken the sun from me;*
> *And my fear is great that you have taken God from me!*

Well, my version of god anyway . . .

Who do I read poetry to now?

Tuesday 28th October

I came back past the hospital today and could see you in my mind's eye. I was half expecting, willing, wishing you to walk towards me with your big dark coat climbing up around your neck, your briefcase swinging in your hand, your beautiful honeyed complexion glowing above your collar, defying all the greyness of this season. You made my heart leap and bounce in my chest. I could hear your voice and the intonation as you said, 'My baby.'

Where do I put all this love I still feel? I want to shower you with it. I'm still in love with you, I'm still in a relationship with you, you are still mine, I still belong to you. Neither of us chose to end this, so where does that leave everything?

Our baby changes every day. I can't tell you how beautiful he is – you would be so proud and happy. He's a piece of heaven, calm, strong and more than I could ever have wished for; he is perfection.

Theo and Otis are thriving. Theo is cracking through his homework without me begging. Otis is now reading beautifully – that happened so fast. They are doing well, they amaze me. I struggle to keep dark thoughts from the door – that something might happen to one of them. I'm writing this down so that it won't happen, so it can never happen. Isn't that what they say, if you declare it, it's less likely to happen?

> When sorrows come they come not as single spies
> But in battalions.

For now, they are fine, safe. I will not infect them with this fear and let it spill over into their lives.

You would fill up, you would be crazed with pride if you could see how well they are doing now.

Theo said tonight, 'I know I can ask other people questions, but no one has infinite knowledge like Dadu.'

Wednesday 29th October

Rex Coltrane Kelly is two weeks old today. I think he was born at 7.25 p.m. He had a terrible night last night – projectile vomiting and squirty diarrhoea. He's exhausted now – I can barely get him to feed. He's my tiny angel. Midwife is coming to weigh him in, pray he has put on weight then maybe we can just revert to boob and no top up. He and I are very in synch.

Thursday 30th October

Feeding Baby Laaa and listening to very loud John Coltrane playing very beautiful, juicy meaty sax. The boys are upstairs getting ready for bed. Everything feels a bit grim tonight.

Oh for sleep! I'm sure you remember this, my love, the only thing that drove you a bit batty about babies I think. So at least I know this would be the situation whether you were here or not, relentless sleep deprivation. I remember when I came back from hospital after having Beanie and you started cooking – that was so lovely. We used to have those crazy dinner parties. Even though we were shattered, we were euphoric too and wanted everyone to meet our little Bean and to celebrate life. People used to pile out of our Shepherd's Bush house at about 3 or 4 a.m. and yet it always felt like we'd just blinked with you around.

I've just put Baby on RH boob so I can't write as easily. I'm going upstairs to read boys a story and Rexy can listen too.

Friday 31st October

I must go and buy many sweets for the other trick or treating children and not eat them all myself before they come.

Darling, I don't know what I'm expecting from writing all this down – that you will come back and read it? The possibility that words on paper might reach you more easily than the thoughts in my head? It's certainly true that I feel dirty and diluted when I try to express anything about you out loud to people apart from Theo or Otis or to your mum, funnily enough. All other conversations lead nowhere. Oh, and Neil – he gets it because he got you so well, I suppose.

Saturday 1st November

Fucking HATE Halloween! Is it an American thing? No wonder you always refused. You thought I was mad dressing them up and letting them ring on people's doors, asking for sweets.

Oh god, Twinx, it was a real low.

Everything's still a bit sore everywhere, post birth sore, arghh, I'm stupid. In the pitch dark with mothers and the odd father from the school trolling down the street, baby strapped across me in a sling and the boys strung out on sugar. I kept losing sight of Otie. Theo knew where he was headed and was with Fin anyway. I couldn't see anything. Somehow we ended up on one of those streets where there's parking on one side and so only enough space for one car to travel up or down at a time. The cars therefore zoom past to get through before they meet another oncoming car.

I am trotting like a lame pony along the pavement, trying to keep up with the kids, 'slinged' baby swinging haphazardly from side to side. I am vaguely worried about him suffocating because I have wrapped him up so warmly against the night and cold. I keep peeling back the folds of the sling and putting my finger underneath his nostrils to check his tiny stream of breath back and forth. Then looking up only to panic because I have lost sight of Otie again. It seems to go on forever. I try to smile and look as if I am having the time of my life so the kids can put this in their memory banks as one of those amazing unforgettable nights . . . Fortunately they barely look back, so caught up are they and their friends in the next booty they can score.

There's a sort of swarm, a colony if you like; nothing ahead of me looks very human. Little homemade antennae are poking up or wizard hats bobbing about and as they all keep swapping accessories it's quite hard to recognise your own. All the adults are watching all the children; it's a collective feeling. At the moment I can't do/be collective – I feel alone, panicked.

The colony does a sharp left across this busy road as a door opens with warm red light emanating from it offering basketfuls of chocolates, I suppose. Otis leaps out into the road after them. I see bright white lights too close and I scream before I even know what's happening. I lurch forward to grab him but feel the sling swing out ahead like a pendulum before me. An arm intercepts and wrenches Otis back to the pavement from the road. Another mother who I've never seen has saved us. The black cab whips past, just clipping the corner of his and my coats. The mother smiles as if this happens all the time and crosses the road with slightly more consideration this time after her own kids.

Everything's heightened after you've given birth – well, everything's heightened after death too I suppose. Perhaps that's it: my nerves are jangled. A simple jaunt like Halloween seems unrepeatable. I never want to feel that again.

Otis seemed remarkably unaware that he was in any danger that evening. Perhaps he was right. Perhaps I'm in my own universe after all. When we got home I suggested it might be fun next year to do it in our house and perhaps spill out into the garden a little . . . if absolutely necessary. They both looked up from their pyramid of sweets, utterly aghast, as if I had missed the whole point of life itself . . .

There was no YOU to hug at the end of this. No big you, that huge trunk of oak-like you to wrap myself around and see where we go. Oh god this is horrible, missing you. 'Missing' is such a pissy hissy little word – it should be a word like 'mammoth'. I am really 'mammothing' you right now – oh, fuck it . . .!

9th November

The last few days have been fairly frantic. I'm never ill, but I caught some feverish cough and cold, which made getting through a normal day like wading through even more treacle. I was sweating and hallucinating. Yes I was. I know I'm an actress but, doctor, I promise I was hallucinating (very slightly). I thought about calling my parents or someone to come and lend a hand, but couldn't bear the thought of 'not being able to cope' so stuck it out, otherwise I would feel even more crappy about myself. I don't think the kids suffered too much. We did drawing and they were allowed loads more computer time, which they always look upon as a bonus. Baby Laaa sucked off a feverish mummy just as thirstily. I love how 'unsqueamish' they are.

I remember with Bops, when I had that mastitis and an abscess grew, it ended up looking like the site of some special-effects moment from a horror film. However pustulating it all was, the midwife would jauntily declare, 'Oh, it'll improve the more you feed!'

'Have you actually had a fucking baby?' I wanted to shout.

And she would inevitably reply, 'Yes, you fool, and I gave him formula the moment he popped out, ha ha, sucker!'

Theo just turned his snub nose slightly to the left and carried on sucking. He's still got two red capillaries tattooed on his cheek from those days of sucking – survival . . . everything in the end, isn't it?

I was thinking this morning how messy and raw pregnancy, birth and the soon afterwards are. It's good I suppose that poetry and fairy tales have always celebrated it and focused on the beauty and joy of it. Imagine if all that was said about childbirth and babies was this . . .

wounds, stitches, engorgement, dripping, chapped bleeding nipples, sleeplessness. For the poor baby there is: discomfort, constant indigestion, somehow still fighting for life even though they've only just been given it! It's all so bloody precarious trying to manage this balance. Is he having enough milk, too much, not enough? Is he growing? Is he alert? Can I make him any more comfortable as he wrestles his little knees up to his tummy to expel that dastard wind again? That little weepy sleep-filled eye that just won't heal. Not all of him is quite ready to function; the symphony is incomplete. The little yelps – which one is for what? Was that wind or was that a smile tracing its way across his face for the first time? God, how I love love love him so – how and why when I'm blind with exhaustion?

. . . would anyone choose to do it if we knew how knife-edged it all felt, how primitive it all is? That's what death is too – desperate and primitive.

I sometimes wonder what the look in your eyes was as you died. How did you die, my love? Did you know? Is that why you left such a wonderful message on my phone minutes before? How can a doctor not know what his body is about to do just before it malfunctions? The world is so blank without you.

I feel very peaceful writing to you. The boys have gone to a 'dog exhibition' with your mum. It's great to have a little space and be able to organise the week. After sorting out play dates, shopping, school stuff, I must get my head into work mode as I'm having a meeting with David and Marleen (*Heaven & Earth*). It seems impossible that I might be discussing something other than Rex or my breasts (which take up far more time than all my children put together at the moment). Who would have thought a body part could get so strung out and demanding! It has an entire eco-system of its own – it doesn't work perfectly all the time, but I marvel at it none the less. I must take Baby for a walk before they close the cemetery in ten minutes.

Saturday 15th November

Rexy is lying across my lap like a beautiful resplendent kitten.

Angel, you are fading from me or rather I'm not summoning you up as effectively as I usually can. You are becoming a memory – it's horrible. Life is striding on without you. There's a momentum that sweeps us up and makes us carry on. I know you would be hugely approving of that, but it feels so casual and impossible. I also know that if I turn my face completely forward it's dishonest. You always have to be there in my line of vision otherwise I'm hiding, pretending everything is dandy. Maybe that is what happiness is – choosing to believe we are well, whether we are or not.

Later

I am checking in with you for strength and courage, my peach. Oh fuck, my crappy character defects. People pleasing – such lies therein hide! I still find myself over-explaining everything to my mum to try and make her a part of everything – well, the integral part of everything she wants or feels she should be. I must learn not to retreat from perhaps disappointing her, to stay true and honest.

I have this fear now that you have gone of being reduced to just 'a daughter', a powerless law-abiding daughter whose only purpose is to obey or disappoint. Even though I might be a creative breadwinner, an organiser, an owner of two houses, a hard-working and loving mother, a good friend to some – a good daughter even? – I still feel this crazy obligation to obey or live by her rules. I struggle to find my own voice, my independence in her presence, I have to hold my ground so as not to be swotted to one side, or so it feels. Perhaps it is true that one is never really set free until our parents die. What a waste, when everyone is just trying their best, I hope it's not true. It's not Mum's fault, it's no one's 'fault', it's just one of the huge lolloping facts one has to accept. It's up to me not to be infantilised. How did you overcome all these quandaries so elegantly in your life?

I have now reached the end of another of your books. It's yet another reminder that I'm further from you than when I started writing this. I am dreading the end of the year, going into next year, 2009, a year in which you will never have lived. Going into a New Year without you by my side. I have known about you, had you in my head, since I was about sixteen, more than half my life, my entire adult life.

You still feel like a heartbeat in the background, the pulse that underlies everything. All things still emanate from you, I dread when that is no longer the case, but perhaps I should attempt to welcome it too.

Your possessions, your office, your computer and music systems will date and break. I suppose you would have replaced them, but for me to do that would be madness. The children's memories of you will fade; a year is such a vast landscape of time for them. Rex will grow and 'Da-da' won't mean very much to him. Your friends are obviously ebbing into the background of our life. The things you taught the boys, they forget, I forget, even the pictures of you fade. All the beautiful things you made wear down and are no longer repairable, it's all of this I dread. I dread letting go of you completely, releasing you, this stage, seeing a balloon get swept up into the sky forever, lost, untraceable.

I still have no idea how you left so quickly, slipped away, you were stolen.

Friday 21st November

Darling, I think I've been letting everything well up for a few days now. I have been looking for a second, a crack in time to squeeze in my tears, my thoughts of you, my desperate desperate longing for you. I can't bear this time elapsing, speeding by, stamping on your smell and fading footprints. If it's possible, the missing you is becoming worse and worse. I keep reminding myself that I had you, so I still have you. You are in me, around us everywhere. I must try to find 'joy' again. I know I will, I know the future will be fine – it's the now that's so difficult, this not daring to think about you for fear of crumpling up.

Thursday 27th November

I just gave baby Rex his last feed. He is an angel. He is definitely life after you. I don't feel sad when I look at him. He fills us with untold joy. His smiles are incredible, they send an electric current through me, a sharp reminder to 'live'. I am not worried about you not being here for him – he will just have a very different life from the other two. I worry about them without you though. You were the lord of their jungle – cross and impatient sometimes, but always this bright shining ball of wisdom for them to hurtle after.

You know, I can't be cross and impatient. I only realise now that we had the luxury to be how we wanted to be. There was always another parent to check and balance, always another person who loved them as much as you or I did. I now feel like the unelected ruler of an island: neither they nor I have any choice.

I must try to sleep . . .

Sunday 30th November

I am getting on a plane to LA with Rexy. I have sold out – I am doing a skincare campaign. I can feel you grinning. You're amused, aren't you? We're going for a couple of days. It will be luxurious. I wish you could come with us; I am going to baptise him in the Chateau Marmont pool!

I have just woken from a nap on the plane, your face there in my mind's eye as I flutter back to life. You made things happen, you made waves, progressed, enthused and infected everyone around you.

The world has already changed so much since you had to go – a 'credit crunch', economic depression, a different season, more terrorist attacks, the Earth's face continuing to burn . . .

Time is striding on, crunching, squelching through every new season. I want to pull it back, scream at it, say, 'What the fuck are you doing?! How dare you leave him behind? We must stay, stay back in those moments where he was still warm, where all hope of him coming back hadn't faded, where we still felt the impact of his actions eddying around us, where the hum of him still reverberated . . .'

I am in a cage, choosing to a degree to be here, to stay here, not to search for a key to let myself out, still scrabbling around for pieces, vestiges of you, of our life together. As well as you, it is 'our life' that I miss, not having anyone to reflect off or beam back to . . .

I don't care about pain. I think I can live with that. It is the urge to progress, discover, be fearless, to risk, that's what I want to keep at the forefront of our lives. Finding the time, the space, the energy to live an engaged life – it's fucking hard on my own with my little sleighful of boys . . .

Does Otis think you will come back? I think he does.

Theo knows but says, 'Nothing is IMpossible, you know?'

Darling, did you know you were going to die?

I want to book an appointment with a heart consultant so that I can understand properly what happened – everything – I want to understand it. I want to be able to explain it to the boys one day if they want/need those kinds of details. Was it even that, *what* in your heart, it all seems so inconclusive? The alternative was impossible though – having your heart cut out and sending it off for a three-week autopsy process. We could not have suspended saying goodbye for that long, or should I have? I just don't know . . . those snap decisions that have to be made twenty-four hours after someone has died – how does anyone make any decision? Or do we make our very best decisions when pushed up against the walls of existence like that?

This is important, that I record this. I don't want to, but I must write it down for the boys . . . I think it was 21st August, looking back at my diaries, but I did screw up the first time we were due to meet. Norman, busiest man on the planet, takes time out to meet me and I forget – maybe that's no accident. Baby, I don't know, I think I'm on top of everything and then I'm really suddenly not. I forget or can't remember huge things and people I know well – their names elude me at critical moments. Anyway, I think that's why I didn't want to record this, I felt terrible about wasting his time. I can hear you lambasting me: 'You don't mess up with Norman. What do you think you're doing?!' He and Liz came the next week, or maybe the 21st was the next week – not sure.

We all went to the hospital, A&E. My legs were jelly. I think Norman and Liz felt sick too.

We went into a corridor first where chairs were lined along the wall. We sat down and they told me the first part. I had already spoken to Adam after you died. I had begged him for a blow by blow account of everything, I wanted every tiny detail. Of course he made it all sound like the perfect way to go. You would have fainted, passed out and not felt any pain, or had any awareness that you were dying. Why then were you lying in the hallway, neatly draped across the floor with one foot holding the front door ajar? I presume because you did know that something catastrophic was happening and, knowing Adam was due to arrive for a drink that you stood a fighting chance of survival if he could gain immediate access to you? I don't know, I can't think about those last few minutes of your life – or I can, but I have no answers. I don't want to start making them up.

Norman said that the ambulance had come very promptly – Adam had obviously been trying to resuscitate you all the while, but had had no response, even though you were still warm when he found you. I keep thinking how utterly horrific this must have been for him, yet I am so so grateful it was him, this brilliant doctor who knew all the methods there were to try and bring you back to life.

Norman was called once you were in hospital, as I remember. I suppose the boys can one day call and ask Adam and the people who were there if they want to. I feel I should put down what I can remember though, as a guide, in case everyone's memory gets stolen . . .

I don't know, I don't know if I can drag up the horror of what I imagine this night must have been. I know random people were involved because of the phone numbers people did or didn't have. No one could reach me because your phone needed a password even though I was the last person dialled when I retrieved the phone – thank god I knew all your passwords.

I just remember Norman then taking me through to the resuscitation room, three empty crisp white beds, with curtains dividing them. There were no patients there whilst we were there. The casualty consultant who had been on call that night was coincidentally there and not run off his feet the day we visited.

He said what had happened – the paddles, crowds of nurses and doctors around you. You were one of their own and a good one at that; they would do anything, just anything to save you. He was unemotional and clear which was very helpful. I sat down by the bed you had lain in. I kept having to remind myself that it was okay, you were already dead, you died in our home not here in this transient no-man's land where so many other people have died and will die. You died with our things, our photos, our smell around you, not here – without the person you chose and the small people you made.

I did imagine it all; I have no idea whether this was cathartic or not. Norman and Liz filled in one another's memories and I know described everything in all the detail they could. They said how extraordinary your mother was. How she went into the room to say goodbye to you once you were pronounced dead. I really don't think I could have done that. Norman said when he arrived there were already so many people gathered, people lined up and down the corridor willing you to come back to life, a strange gathering, a sort of 'protest' I suppose. He rushed past them (knowing him, he was probably already pushing up his sleeves to get stuck in, refusing to believe you had died yet).

He sat on the chair next to me as he was describing this. He was wearing his glasses. He's tough, Norman, terrier tough, he's a fighter, and however much he fought his emotion in these moments, as happens to me, it kept bubbling over making itself visible. He told me he shouted as he entered this resuscitation room. Something along the lines of, 'Come on, just cut him open.' Apparently it's called a thoracotomy? Liz said he was so desperate to get to you, wrench you back into life again. He said he realised quickly once he had more information that all hope was lost. Typical though that he refused to give up on you, wasn't it? I was thinking in that moment how like you he was: you would have screamed the hospital down to save his life too.

The general surgeon told me that they tried well beyond the time they knew it was over, just pulling out all the stops, in case a miracle might happen. Even doctors who have all this knowledge rely on that possibility in the end. There's a lot of comfort in that, as I know the boys think about miracles happening too.

They then showed me the room where you were laid to rest, where people could go one by one and pay their last respects.

Norman joked that at the LPSA meeting earlier on that evening everyone had been commenting on how well you looked – 'good-looking bastard . . .'.

Adam said the same when he found you. 'He was peaceful, healthy, tanned, good-looking.'

I look around this aeroplane and there are all these men who are older than you. They don't look happy – how can they not? They can still breathe. Are you out there amongst these fluffy clouds, smiling into our frosty window?

Our baby beams. You would burst with pride.

Later

I was thinking about *Heaven & Earth*, about playing this incredible character who displays the same determination and finesse as you, perhaps without your grace though.

She grabs hold of all that might hurt in life, welcomes every challenge, steps out of every possible comfort zone in exactly the way you did. She lets nothing pass or go to waste. She ploughed through every obstacle, looking upon life as a battlefield, quite exhausting. What a gift this part will be if it all happens; I can't quite believe it. It is as if you have a conch and are channelling some path for us to follow, gently guiding us back into life, into activity, keeping us steady.

I am surrounded by a great deal of fortune. To have a house that we own, resources, great friends, parents who love me, all this AND our three treasures.

Is it possible to live with the loss of you and feel happiness?

Can mood be as simple as perception? Do we have a choice about how we feel? I think you did. Your life as it becomes distilled seems so pure. It was lived with such purpose and guidance. You surmounted obstacles so quickly they seemed not to exist. You did at least one thing you really didn't want to do every day.

I still live with this delusion that if I could just be still, not have to *do*, if I could stare out of the window and dream, or eat or sleep or be inert as the sun heated me, that all that would make me terribly happy. Whereas time and again it is activity that brings me fulfilment and reward. It's the same for the kids. When will I realise this? Not to hearken after stillness but to ride the wave and be willing to be tossed about by it, ruffled up? Well, all this has surely done that . . .?

I search for your opinion in every action I take. I even assess new people, wondering what you would make of them. I tell Rexy things about you. I tell him most fervently that his Dadu would love to nestle in the back of his neck and inhale the scent of his fragile little egg head.

I swam in the pool at the Chateau. I took Baby in. It was a bit bloody cold, but I held him tight to keep him hot, and as with everything else, he took it all in his stride . . .

I have written so many other things. It is remarkable how repetitive I am in these diaries. I have never read over my diaries before and now I am having to confront how dull they are. I've written about the people in my life, the places we go, literally how things seem, but I can't be bothered to transcribe any of this. I only want to scoop my hand around in this water well to see if there's anything left of you. I'm in a panic that it will all dry up any day now. All that you need to know from everything I am leaving out is that I'm pushing Heal here, there and everywhere, I'm convinced something will come of it sometime, something will come from all these investments you made, from all of your endeavours.

The Kid has resurrected itself, not sure if it will happen. I won't do anything on it until I do know. There's still no definitive news on *Heaven & Earth*, which is frustrating as I will have so much work to do on it if/when it does come together.

I am going straight to Otie's carol concert when we land, then we're having 'mummy and him' time (Theo's at Charlie's).

We are landing in a minute. Little Rex is lolloped in my arms making noises like a squeaky rubber toy.

I've missed the boys these last few days. We've been Skyping. Otie took the computer to bed – he went under his duvet and shone a torch into his face so I could still see him, delicious boy.

Oh fuck . . . I don't know what I'm doing really, floundering all over the place. I can't be bothered to go into the details, only things get so fucking hard sometimes. I have no clue why I think they should not be hard – where did I pick up that expectation? I must remember our adage:

'Work hard. Expect nothing. Celebrate!'

Wednesday 17th December

It was my birthday on Sunday. That was an incredibly hard day on this planet without you.

From about last Wednesday to Sunday was hard, I missed you terribly. I took out some of our friends who have been so amazingly supportive since you died.

All day long I was so emotional at having lost our life, desperately trying to shove grief away, wade through it – but its pull was like quicksand and suddenly I'd be halfway deep in it again, not knowing how the hell I had got there. You can't run, can't hide, unless you want to lie or live in a cocoon. I remember the first poem you wrote to me. You called it 'Cocoon' – it made my heart fly and sway like a kite. Twelve years ago was that? Your imprint still seems vital to me, like the way two colours mix together on a palette, where no two others make quite the same colour. We had a colour together and without you here to add your colour it has become this stagnant shitty brown!

Where were you on my birthday celebration night? There was an air of expectation. I think we all hoped that you might somehow appear.

I was so spoilt with you. Life was riveting, so full, bursting with possibilities. I could listen to you talk for hours and hours. No more talking from you or to you . . . that's purgatory.

I had a rough weekend with the kids. I shouted on Saturday morning and bloody well started to cry in the middle of it. What an ass I am. I didn't stop; I finished what I had to say. It was along the lines of . . . Well, I should go back.

Otis shouted at me asking why I always had to take so long. (We were getting ready to go for a bike ride in the cemetery.) It was taking ages because my time as usual had been spent preparing all their things to go out, finding helmets etc, cleaning up after breakfast. I then had to run back upstairs to grab my coat. It had already been a morning where nothing satisfied him, nothing was good enough – he was ranting a fair bit. I was trying to keep it light, trying to praise all the good he was doing, all the usual tricks. Something snapped inside me when he accused me of keeping them waiting. Unfortunately Baby was crying in his pram and the various noise levels were riding high.

I blurted: 'Do you know what I've been busy doing? Getting everyone ready, it takes time, maybe you could help get some things ready too then it would all take less time, we have to help each other.' My voice then rose. 'I am human, I have feelings too!' Then I said something about you and how I knew you having gone upset him so and it upsets me too, I can't remember exactly as that's when my voice started to crack and I became more emotional. Theo turned to face the wall and Otis quietened and stared at me. Once I had finished my rant, he then really didn't want to come out.

We walked through the cemetery and I talked and said I was sorry for raising my voice but sometimes I had to make my position clear; I can't be their slave.

Theo turned to me and said, 'The problem is Otie knows Dadu is dead, but he doesn't know what that means.' I have to say I think that was fairly bang on.

Friday 19th December

There is no place on earth where death cannot find us ... We do not know where death awaits us: so let us wait for it everywhere. To practise death is to practise freedom. A man who has learned how to die has unlearned how to be a slave.

Kim sent me her favourite Montaigne quotes on my birthday. I'll put them all in at some point.

You're not around, are you? I write to you, but gradually it's not to you. I know you're not getting any of this. It is like an echo that is bouncing back at me far too quickly to have ever been heard.

Have I said goodbye? It doesn't feel as if you are here any more. You have gone, haven't you? That was so quick. I long to turn it all around, be there when your heart skipped a beat and yes, my darling, fucking save you!

Christmas Day (in cottage)

I think the kids had a fantastic day. Mum and Roy were amazing. Roy rustled up a fantastic Christmas lunch with very little help from any of us, whilst I was able to really BE with the kids taking the odd break for baby and boob. They had very cool presents from me this year – no, from *us*, they had lovely presents from us. Baby was a little unsettled. I assume it was his tummy, but I'm really not sure.

I went for a walk with my mum and Rex and we spoke about you. The sky was perfectly clear, blue and crisp. There was a bird of prey circling over our heads and I hoped it was you sending rushes of love my way.

Life is functioning and functioning fairly well, but the juice, the glitter, the vibration is lost in you. I try not to think about you all the time because I 'function' better when I don't. I was sentimental in the cards I wrote to the boys, but then that felt right; not to acknowledge your absence would have been so strange.

We had a glass of champagne before lunch. I dragged everyone into your 'tryphidy' greenhouse for an aperitif. I mixed elder-flower and sparkling water for Otie and Theo. It made us think of you being in that gorgeous green place, you potting and planting banana plants that would continue to grow after your death and burst through the roof! I bought Otie some Christmas tree seeds to plant so that when he's ten he'll be able to choose one of his very own trees to be our Christmas tree.

A few days ago Matthew took the boys out and bought me an iTouch (Theo's suggestion) as a Christmas present from them, a very snazzy one that I have no idea how to use. He is so thought-ful. I'm very lucky with these wonderful friends I have.

No longer being 'special' for someone (hate that word), not being someone's 'person' will be so hard. It's as strange the other way – not having that one person, you, to give love to. I suppose that energy can change, get transmitted in other ways – are the boys getting more love and attention from me than before? I hope so. Shouldn't that be the natural order of things – if they have lost one parent they need more from the other one?

It seems cruel that my time with them will inevitably be cut in two since I must work twice as much as before to compensate for the loss of your income, just at the time they need me twice as much. These kinds of conundrums or equations make my heart sweat. There's suddenly an anxiety and a feeling that I won't make it, that all of this may soon unravel.

> When we get out of the glass bottles of our own ego,
>
> . . .
>
> we shall shiver with cold and fright
> but things will happen to us
> so that we don't know ourselves.

Cool, unlying life will rush in,
And passion will make our bodies taut with power,
. . .

Ha! I LOVE that poem. I immediately feel anything is possible as long as I remain open to possibility . . .

Boxing Day

There is this . . . this ebbing away of you. The truth is starting to glare at me, it's brighter, more insistent. There is no father for my children – that part would outrage you. You exist; even if it's only my version of you somewhere inside of me, you must exist. This next phase feels as if you are sinking to the bottom of me rather than your head bobbing to the surface every day. I want to wrench you to the surface to be with you, on this paper, on DVDs, pictures, any which way. At some point you become a part of history – when does this tip into that? How can you only exist in the past, part of what was and not what *is*? You created so much, there was no hesitation in you, you saw what needed doing and pounced, you learned so much. All that knowledge stored in your fantastic brain, has it just disintegrated, evaporated?

Doesn't love have to live, have to be fed like us, in order to survive? The furnace from your love might still be embers by the time I die, this is true . . .

Can one really go on loving a dead person? I think I can, but is that loyalty, is that being in love with what we *had*? You see, I want to hold you, smell you, bury my head in your chest again, stroke the back of your head, kiss you. I miss your heat in the night.

I like being alone, so that part could continue until I die – what I don't like is this 'one-legged' family. I want the boys to have a father. I feel inadequate and perfectly enough for them all at once.

The point to remember I suppose is that my parenting would be imperfect even if you were alive.

Amanda and Mark had their Boxing Day party with masses of food and generosity. Theo and Otis going ballistic and in ecstasy slugging Coke, glued to PlayStations – they wanted to stay forever.

I'll just be 'coping' with the kids so much of the time. Just doing that – trying to keep them happy, contented, occupied, thriving – all that is a great deal of work. Why wouldn't it be?

Tuesday 30th December

The year where you were still here is coming to an end.

I was watching Baby this morning lying next to me in bed and he started smiling at the blank wall, even though there were plenty of other distractions like fairy lights to look at. He smiled seemingly at nothing. He often does this and of course he's closer to not being alive (having recently come to life) than any of us, so I imagine perhaps he already met you in those few months where you overlapped at your end and his very beginning? You would love him so much – his smile splits his face open just like yours used to, he must have caught it from you during the crossover. What other treasures did you load him up with?

I went for a long walk yesterday, our favourite one along the meadows. I was on my own for the first time in such a long while. The day was spectacular, sharp blue skies, shards of sunlight and absolutely no one around. I talked out loud to you. I sat down on one of those huge logs and looked up at you. When I talk to you, you are wearing something. Yesterday you were wearing your bulky lumberjack shirt and when I talk to you I cry. I suppose I reignite our relationship from my side. There's no one to join, to finish a sentence, retort, mock, applaud, so your absence becomes stronger yet I meet you, I make some very sane connection, it's a strange double act.

I LOVE YOU.

Saturday 3rd January, back in London

I am amazed to be sitting down with a pen in my hand and a second's peace . . . Heaven . . .

Rexy has just fallen asleep because I pegged around the cemetery with him in his pram and have left him unmoved for fear he may wake and start squawking again. He's not sleeping very much any more, so it is a real challenge to get anything done, from changing a light bulb to changing my clothes. I think I have now been wearing the same clothes for days on end – I hang them on the end of the bed at night and pull them on in the morning until there's a moment when Rexy falls asleep and the boys are safely occupied and I race like a madwoman to have a shower and pull something clean out of the wardrobe. Oh the mundanity of it all! It keeps me trudging forward I suppose. These little precious segments of time precariously apportioned to each task keep our boat afloat.

It seems crazy, but I have to be up by 5 a.m. to keep on top of everything. I washed my hair this morning for the first time in a week, hoping no one would wake. I felt like a thief, a time thief. My angel, this is just the 'surviving' bit – god only knows how I get to the 'living' again. The thoughts, hopes, dreams belong to another existence for the moment. The last words that float about in my head as I fall to sleep are:

load, unload
dishwasher
search Theo PSP
clothes still in washer
Ocado
thank you letters
arrange
play date
insurance form

birthday present
bank
call electrician
septic
tank
logs
sew labels
school trip
lunchbox
check Natwest file
piano
kids' dentist
must read more with Oti
baby inoculations . . . forgot
must sleep
grab s l e e p
fix O t i e's bike
h e l . . .

Saturday 10th January

Sophie has come into our lives! You liked her when she came to give the boys French lessons. She's lovely, calm and kind. She speaks only in French to baby Rex, the idea being if he wants to speak it there is at least the same opportunity the other two had with you around. The boys seem happy with her, still slightly annoyed that there has to be anyone else, though. It is SO much more manageable. I have an assistant – that's what it feels like. She's so helpful and willing and understands bereavement only too well.

I will finally get some work done next week. The drip drip of ideas is just beginning. I need some space to allow it to percolate. I want to read everything about Barry, and read the script over and over again.

Can I play a convincing man? You always said I had a bum like a peach, could that be a disadvantage, I wonder . . .?

My lack of sex life should help. When I eventually stop breast feeding, I will feel quite asexual, I think, and I'll bring that to the forefront too. I am strong, I have resolve, I have a huge well of grief for all that's gone. I can use all these elements, all is not lost, it's never too late to prepare; she's in me somewhere. This is the kind of role I have pined for my whole life and it's finally come along, a gift, a new journey to go on.

Last night the boys and I watched some of the footage you had filmed of them as babies. We lay draped across one another under our duvet. I have slowly been taking all our cameras to Charlie's edit suite and salvaging any footage that's lying around, having him put it on DVDs so the kids can watch it whenever they like. Afterwards Theo seemed pensive – he has such a beautiful mind and Otis said that he wanted to squeeze whatever or whoever killed you. For myself, I just wanted to squeeze YOU again and again. We are off to Alba's house for lunch, laden with crêpes and Nutella in honour of you and your Frenchness . . .

Thursday 14th January

I start shooting four weeks from tomorrow.

I had Lauly around for dinner last night. She wants to finish all the music you were working on together. I feel very passionately that she should too. She's asking Magnus and Jim whether they can get involved. I would love for it to be ready for your memorial in May.

As I woke up this morning, I heard a soft male voice emanating from the sitting room. I was hugely comforted by it. Instead of a sharp inhalation, my first breath of the day was a relaxed exhalation.

Perhaps I'm no longer alone with my chimps in the jungle? I thought for a split second it was you. It's only in that space between waking and sleep that I can see, hear or feel you. It was Roy – Mum and Roy had stayed the night. Mum was being the perfect maternity nurse. I have slept – I feel as if I have rocket fuel coursing through my veins!

Tuesday 27th January

I haven't written to you for a while, my angel. Perhaps it will stop all together one day – there will no longer be a need for it. Just the thought of that makes my eyes sting and my throat tighten. I have been fine for a while. I feel a tiny pang of guilt about that, about being fine. I read this recently:

Still, there's no denying in some sense I 'feel better', and with that comes at once a sort of shame, and a feeling that one is under a sort of obligation to cherish and foment and prolong one's unhappiness. I've read about that in books, but I never dreamed I should feel it myself.

It's from C. S. Lewis's *A Grief Observed*. He shares so many wonderful insights, but I can't help losing track when he refers everything back to God. Perhaps I'll suffer more in my cynicism?

I miss you so much physically at the moment. Now that I am winding up breast feeding, my hormones are changing, I'm no longer a lactating bovine creature. I'm human, I'm female, I'm without a mate. There is no one like you. I think in an abstract way I might find you again.

When I write to you, connect with you, I feel whole again, pure, right in myself. Maybe this is delusional, staying in this cage, safe with memories of you, avoiding anything new. However, when I don't write to you, I very quickly become disconnected, wobbly, not only emotionally but also in terms of what really matters.

I read something in my James Barry research, which I found terrifying but inspiring:

You must always be able to account for every hour in the day.

That is how you lived your life – valuing every hour. I can't help starting to live my life as you lived yours, circumstances force me to, but also a desire to make up for your loss – I know that is impossible. To be like you, that will never happen, but it feels exhilarating borrowing your behaviour, practising your personality. At some point I have to come back to myself – even the parts I hate – to be who I am rather than live in your wake.

I have a vivid memory, which hasn't seemed relevant until now. You were standing framed in our bedroom window. It was very early in the morning. I said something along the lines of:

'I just don't know what I would do if anything were to happen to you, if you died.'

It was a moment where I loved you so much the drama queen in me went straight to the other end of the spectrum, the 'not having you' end. You said, and I'm fairly sure this is accurate as it has stuck with me:

'Well, you would live on and you would love again.'

I remember being shocked.

'Oh god, I couldn't. Would you really?'

'Yes, of course,' you said effortlessly. 'What is life without love?'

I vaguely remember us rolling around on the bed for a while, you laughing with mock repulsion, vigorously denying you would ever be able to have sex with anyone else. We never moved on to my side of that story.

Darling, if I find – I can't even say it – if I am lucky enough to be handed another portion of happiness and love even, what happens to us? How do you exist for me? You are half Basque – you would go fucking nuts if anyone laid a finger on me. Just imagine if you came back, what calamity! I would have betrayed you! I know the logical answers to these questions, but I am not interested in those. I want to know: does your spirit die if I don't keep blowing air into it?

Thursday 12th February, Cape Town

I have been cracking the whip on myself, getting ready to play James Barry, so haven't written at all. We have been here for ten days, rehearsing, riding, training, learning how to ride a pony and trap, shoot a nineteenth century gun, speak Xhosa and play chess. How absurdly privileged is my job?

Friday 13th February, Cape Town

We were meant to start shooting *Heaven & Earth* today. It seems the money isn't all in place. The story seems fairly straightforward, but who really knows if it's the whole truth or not? We find out tomorrow if we are going to start shooting on Sunday. I am grateful for these few extra days. As Orla suggested, I can just take a day to be 'him' all day. I feel I can't quite do that – I'm not sure if that's fear of falling short of this mammoth role or just having too many expectations.

Monday 16th February

Rex and I are about to arrive back in London. The film has fallen through, which feels impossible. All the sets were ready, costumes sewn together, actors rehearsed and ready, but no cameras to roll on it all – it was very strange. Pierce is going to see if his production company can come in and join – we are going to work through a list of potential producers and financiers. I think I have to behave as if it's over even though I'll continue to do everything I can to make it happen.

I had relaxed financially, thinking this job would take care of some problems. I have to look upon this as an opportunity; it already feels like it might be. What is the point of disappointment? It doesn't help anything at all. The film will either come together at some point or *The Kid* will happen or maybe even something through my US agent. I haven't heard from them for an age, so who knows . . .?

Marleen turned out to be wonderful and I would love to work with her again one day. She's so compassionate and passionate; she lives and breathes the story.

Friday 20th February

I am down in the cottage. The boys had one of those spectacular days where they spent the entire day outside, dawn till dusk. It felt as if it might possibly be the first day of spring. It was everything you would have wanted – all of it – just how you would have loved a day down here, with your little baby boy as the new addition. He's so cute. The only word for him right now is 'cute' – that's what Theo calls him. 'Mumble, he's too cute, he needs to go to jail for cuteness offences!'

You would live burrowed in his neck and he would chew your fingers and knuckles. He sits up now, ramrod straight with his perfect sashimi tongue poking out, panting like a puppy.

I want to kiss, to feel intimacy, to hold, be held and lose myself in a night wrapped up in sheets with a man's body, a body that might well be a duplicate of yours.

I still love you, but you not being here makes that increasingly difficult – what do I love now? Everything you were, the pieces you jigsawed into our sons?

Would I be betraying you or is it natural now to want to hold someone?

You are my reality, my journey. Everything we've created is still here, except you – what does one do with that? Yes, I want to keep your spirit, your legacy, alive, but I need to bring something new to life as well, however peripheral. Would it be like a 'long weekend' from my reality, a break? Then what happens? Does that break become a week, two weeks, a month? And if it's longer than that then where are you? How do you fit in? You are no longer the reality and that is unacceptable somehow.

Friday 27th February

I am finding less and less time to write.

You used to always say you had a physical need for sex and intimacy; you were like a plant without water if you didn't have that in your life. I never really thought about it. I suppose it was all so easy. I had you; I took that for granted – how readily available you were all the time, completely up for it, whenever, however. I remember you saying jokingly once or twice that I didn't realise how lucky I was always having someone so attracted, so desiring of me – many people don't have that in their marriages. Fuck, I didn't know how right you were. I don't want to shut that side of myself down forever. I don't only want to experience mother love. God, I sound so fucking spoilt. I have to say what's going on, it's like a confession. I feel sweaty just writing this stuff down. I would never look beyond you if you were here. The way you can stop me thinking like this is to come back!

I want to be held, I want to have sex, to be inspired by another human being. I want to look deeply into someone's eyes and have him if I can't have you. I want that frantic moment before it all kicks off, the rush, the excitement, the spin, that language . . . I miss it.

A wise woman said to me that after the death of your love you will feel so many contradictory things . . .

'You won't experience this for a while because you are pregnant. However, don't be surprised how the desire for sex will hit you like a freight train, like never before. You want to experience sex because you need to check that you yourself are still alive.'

I never fully grasped that sex and death cliché, but it seems to be true. I feel a huge urge to shake off grief. I want to be light, I want to be physical with someone if I can't be physical with you.

I have a complete horror of showing this body you loved so blindly to anyone else though. The havoc that has been wreaked upon it is *our* havoc, our work, what we wanted to make together inside of it; I was our kiln. I welcomed that – I didn't care a damn what happened because I had you to love me.

I love you so much, but I can't HAVE you.

What would happen if I tried to sleep with someone else? Would you circle about us and cast some potent spell?

'NO ONE shall enter my woman!'

I'm laughing and crying at the hopelessness and hopefulness of all this . . .

I need to write my tribute for your memorial. Arghh, I can't – what is there to say? I'm working on your gravestone. I found someone lovely to do it through Suzy Murphy – he's a sculptor. I think it might be fabulous, can a gravestone be fucking fabulous? Anyway, it shall be the shape of a rocket – don't laugh, I promise it's not a phallic symbol. You'll see when it's ready – just look up from where you are lying now . . .

9th March

I wish I could think of the perfect epitaph for you to put on your gravestone.

My body aches for you. It was all so easy, so right. Our pups would be tucked up in bed. I don't know why they never came in on us, but even if they had, how lovely to see their parents together, loving, the way they were meant to be.

If I find this with someone else now, what, what is it? Is it constant insecurity for them, fear of not being you? Fear that these three little strangers might not accept them, a sadness about 'inheriting' someone else's woman? Or is it possible to start again enriched from everything I shared with you? Could I now be better, kinder, more tolerant, compassionate, grateful than I was before? Would this man in fact be the lucky one?

You had to put up with all the growth, the shit. We've now trained one another how to be in a relationship. You taught me how to give and receive love. Would I be able to give more this time, take a bit less, because I arrive with my tank still half full from you? I would come with a ready made family, full of potential. Nothing has been broken or shattered. It was ended too abruptly, you and love were torn away from us, but there's no betrayal; our idea of love remains intact. I think the four of us believe in love – it has only ever fed us, made us happy. Why wouldn't we want to experience it all over again? Fuck, as you always said, I can convince myself and anyone else of just about anything.

As I'm writing this, that track from *Beyond Skin*, 'Letting Go', has just come on. I listen to Nitin Sawhney all the time, the only music I don't crumble to.

Your memorial – this huge date lumbering towards us – I want it to show *you*, really show who you were. I'm half afraid of diving deeply back into you, being intimate, going through all our footage to find material for the tribute, photos of you, long lost ones, your contributions, unearthing everything. I must though – there is just no possibility of not having fireworks for you, no possibility of you 'drifting out' – that will never happen.

Thursday 11th March

God darling, I don't know what to write any more. What can I say? You are not here to say it to. I can't bear for you to fade, not to keep colouring you in, not to keep you in bold print. I'm becoming so repetitive. Is this the process – **keep repeating until it finally sinks in –** until I become so bloody annoying I have to stop?

I feel so shallow at the idea of 'moving on'. What does that imply, that you have been left behind somewhere? No, you haven't; you are streets ahead. Perhaps I have not accepted any of what has happened, which is why I feel life is manageable or am I so shallow that I can bounce back? There will be help along the way. There is a message embedded in all of this somewhere.

If I gave my heart to someone else, would you be there at the end? Would I still be buried on top of you in the cemetery? Why does that bring a lump to my throat, the loss of that privilege? Would I still be yours in death if I can no longer be that in life?

I don't want to ever abandon you.

Fuck, I wasn't there when you died.

It suddenly feels like a lifetime ago. How could I not have been there? Maybe that was your last gift to us: none of us would have made it if we had witnessed your death.

I've just opened my email and put your name into the search of my inbox file and found some old emails between us. It all feels tangible again for a minute, soft and warm, just like this writing to you. This is the only time I don't feel stretched and harassed. It's like a meditation of sorts, these incantations, confessions I make to you. It's strange to revisit these emails when there is no longer an address to reply to.

Theo was looking over my shoulder the other day as I was about to use Skype. The addresses are listed along the left hand side of the screen – yours still resides in first place. Theo said, 'Quick, click on "Martin Kelly". Go on, let's just see what happens.'

'Nothing will happen. I already tried it once,' I said.

'Go on, I just want to see . . .'

Up on the screen pinged 'User not found'.

'Never mind,' he said kindly, plucking at the skin around his fingernails.

Our beautiful soulful boy . . .

★

I want to close the casket, put the lid down, stop rifling around, delving into your wonderfulness. I need to try and find some other kind of wonderfulness. It goes so quickly, as you always said. How did you know that? I do and desperately don't want to look back. I want to honour everything. I want to give it the place it deserves – you in a Byzantine frame battered together from the softest most precious gold to preserve you forever.

I am itching to live, to escape this loss, this you, this love that has to be a memory. It is not enough; death is final. No, it is not just final, it's worse than that, it's diminishing: the dead continue to decrease, to occupy less space, very obviously I suppose. They don't need clothes, they don't order on Amazon, they don't consume, they don't argue or come up with any new ideas. They don't demand time or space – only those who are living and have loved them demand that. We demand that they are spoken of regularly, pictured along mantelpieces and walls and repeatedly dragged into the forefront of our minds. Until we reach a time when we are exhausted from blowing air into a balloon that deflates faster and faster each time. It becomes a desperate, soul-destroying exercise – one has to turn away to look for something that is breathing, growing, that might possibly last . . .

Survival is brutal.

I need to be brutal.

Rex claws at me, clings with fists and nails so tightly. He's a tiny savage Buddha. He will hang off the skin on my cheek or neck, it makes no difference to him – not falling, that is all that matters. His grip is as tenacious and ferocious as it needs to be. He has to hang on to survive. He knows he can't stand or walk; he knows he's dependent. I have to stand and walk and know I am independent.

I cannot rely on you for anything now.

You have honoured us, taken care of us, made sure that we can keep our home – the most mundane, unspectacular set of form filling would have had to be endured – I have just done the same for the boys – it was a huge act of selflessness – thank you, you have provided for us, even in your death.

I miss everything you brought to me, to us, to them, and, yes, it is in us, around us, all your gifts, but they are only extensions of you, the branches and not the tree. You are not here.

Do you know that yet?

Will I ever know that?

Perhaps it is not something I have to know or accept. I can live alongside it until it catches up with me, the thud of acceptance, when all I want to do is scream NO, IT CANNOT BE!

> Soldier, scholar, horseman, he,
> . . .
> As 'twere all life's epitome.
> What made us dream that he could comb grey hair?
>
> W. B. Yeats

That's your epitaph, that's what I'll put on your gravestone – it is almost perfect, isn't it?

17th March

I think about you – no, I don't think about you. You are in my head, pictures of you, your look, I still don't understand where the hell you can be . . .

Does grief or loss or not having the love of your life any more leave you more open? Is there a crucial moment of openness or 'availability' before you seal closed like a clam and become ossified and no one even wants to try and get in any more?

Perhaps I am horribly open, obvious, available at the moment and I don't even know. Maybe I'm giving off some kind of gamma ray like a tropical fish, some strange vibration? Or will I never be able to do that again? Perhaps I no longer have that encoded into me, did you take all my secret codes with you to the grave? I still have yours – I know you – I can't read a map, but I could read every synapse in you.

If I lay myself open to someone, am I betraying you? I can't fucking 'date'! Putting aside the impossibility of time (it would have to take place between 11 p.m.–4 a.m. at the moment), how do I date? It's not even whether someone might like me, it's our brood –

'Is there anyone out there who would like to adopt a brood, one of them freshly baked?'

Qualifications
- **You have to be young so there's a hope you won't die any time soon, please.**
- **You love being with kids but strangely have none of your own, or if you do, you want three more and will love them unconditionally . . .**
- **The mother's an actress. I know they are generally a fucking nightmare, but I think she's been fairly humbled by recent events.**
- **She's probably done enough procreating.**
- **She is self-sufficient and survives financially as long as she doesn't have to support you too . . .**
- **She needs to work hard and spends all her time when not working with her children so won't actually have any time to spend with you.**
- **She is an insomniac and doesn't shut up.**

That would all have to be honestly declared on the front side of the tabard as I advertise myself along Oxford Street, passing by confused-looking foreign-language students. On the back would be written:

In return she will make you feel the most loved and adored you have ever been. A 'king of love' a 'love god'!

That isn't much compensation is it? Would you have me second-hand?

Oh, COME BACK.

It is very selfish of me, but I don't want our loss of you to define our lives. I want the alive you, the you we talk about, the you that makes our boys who they are – that's the defining *you*.

How long does grieving last, is it forever? Look at me trying to fudge together a new life without you. I won't rush, but I want to. I think I have the courage to withstand this emptiness, pain, loneliness, confusion, whatever it is. I know where my salvation lies – in mothering, in doing this, acting whenever I'm invited to – it's this activity, not another person, that will help complete this half-circle.

Can I just talk to you once more, that's all?

23rd March

I am finding it difficult to commit or settle into anything at the moment. I am very scattered. I am not helping myself – my organisation has gone out the window. I have lost all discipline. I have had too many late nights. I'm living like a student, having friends over, drinking much wine, empty packets of cigarettes lying in dustbins and three hours' sleep a night between the baby wakes. What am I doing? Trying clumsily to grab at the coat tails of something we used to do? Something that was sustainable with two adults and two children but is clearly not with one adult and three children . . .

I am going to the theatre with Mum and Roy tonight to see *Burnt by the Sun*. I pray I keep my eyes open. All I want to do is sleep.

INSERT:

Postscript to that: no chance of my eyes closing – they were

prised open much further. It was absolutely brilliant. Such wonderful performances – I was transported.

I have made one commitment in an attempt to reassemble order. I
will not Skype or call anyone or answer or send any emails after 10.30
p.m. I think that's what's killing me, staying up to the wee small hours
just trying to cover everything off in a rather ineffectual way.

I met Wim on Friday (the sculptor who will make your gravestone). He is lovely – Tom Hammick-ish – you would like him. I
am still swinging all over the place as to what to put on your gravestone – the kids and I talk about it. We thought about symbols
from us all, the pieces of you now in us I suppose.

Oh god, there is nothing enough for you. Obviously this isn't a
summary of your life, but I don't know, it has to be there forever,
it has to make sense as the boys grow up. I don't want them to feel
embarrassed about anything on your grave. I want it to be timeless,
as you now are. I want them to be able to visit you on the important
days of their lives. Can you imagine when or if they get married to
the person of their dreams or if they have a baby they can come
and tell you about these spectacular things? They can bring their
new people to you, literally have a cornerstone, something to
clutch on to that represents our feelings for you. They can tell you
about their lows, they will have somewhere to divulge any dark-
ness, a secret place with just you listening in the breeze, no raised
voices to disagree. Imagine, you don't ever have to be the law
maker – you have already broken all the rules. I want them to feel
pride, a swell in their hearts, and a knowledge that under there is
someone who is all theirs, who will always love them whatever
happens, however wayward we might become.

Wednesday 8th April, Duved, Sweden

We're in Hotell Duvedsgården again. Thank god they didn't put us
in the same room as last year. Baby is back home with Noni and

Roy. Theo had a slight meltdown when we arrived. I was cross with him for kicking the door in frustration because he couldn't get his suitcase through the door. He didn't hear me and went on kicking. I blurted out: 'If Dadu was here, he would be shocked. Look at what you are doing . . .!'

He shouted back, crawled under the bed and hid.

What the fuck was I thinking? Well, that's the point. I wasn't thinking. I was just reacting like another child. What possessed me to use your name as a way of disciplining them when you are not here? I have not felt the urge to do that throughout the last year, only to do the opposite and tell them how proud you would be of this or that. I think I've destroyed all the nurturing in one fell swoop. So bloody clumsy of me. I am so angry with myself.

You were incredibly present here yesterday when we all walked in without you, the same hosts' faces to greet us, minus you. I desperately wanted to show them Baby, to hold him up as our new fourth person:

'Look, all's not lost – look, we sowed the seeds of THIS before he died! Please, please don't look sad. We are here to have fun, fun, fun!'

Instead I smiled broadly and preoccupied myself with the five boys Lucy and I herded into the lobby. Kids spare no time for people's questions.

We all went dog sleighing last night. (It's just Lucy and her three boys. Al is teching his play and couldn't come in the end.) We had dinner in the hut in the middle of the forest again. All the kids detested the dinner and Sven the dog-sleigh man (same one as last year) proudly declared that to his knowledge no child had ever eaten a morsel of his food – they all hated it. I winced slightly as I realised those were five of the seven heads we were paying for.

I only realised how INSANELY extravagant you were again when we got the bill. The dog-sleighing bit was AMAZING, though. Lucy was at the helm of our sleigh doing a brilliant job as I clutched on to some of our brood, and dog-sleigh man took the others.

Charles Butler is going to join us today. Another one who

adored you. I feel terribly responsible as there is nothing here, no scene, no particular vibe. I hope that works as well for him as it does for us.

Easter Sunday, 12th April

We have just had a massive Easter egg hunt with all the boys down in the basement of the hotel. Charles has been great playing with them, teasing them, a reminder, a piece of you in all that somewhere. I think he's the friend you have known the longest – were you twelve?

I went for the most spectacular ski yesterday. Lucy guided us through forests, all silent, crunchy and beautiful. I couldn't stop thinking about you.

The boys were each allowed to spend a night in my bed because with no baby around sleep has become less of a precious commodity. Otie fell out and banged his beautiful little face. He didn't even wake as I hauled him back into bed. In the morning he was sporting a black eye! He loves it and is already worried that it might fade before we get back to London and he won't be able to show it off. Theo's nose exploded in the night – all the bed sheets and towels are strewn with blood. It looks like a Tarantino set in here. He's so casual and unflappable about that stuff now.

Charles is leaving this morning. It was great having him for a couple of days. He has this practised light-hearted approach to everything. He is almost disparaging of you at times, but in that upper-class English way where he means just the opposite of whatever he is saying.

He then said something that took my breath away. He prefers seeing us here rather than in London because, 'Quite frankly, when I come to the house in London, I feel as if I could burst into tears.' I was so glad he had the balls to say that, simply because I now know he holds you in the same esteem and affection as you always held him. Like someone you have known for most of your life, I know there was a deep visceral understanding between the two of you, the boys pick up on it. They trust him completely and hurl themselves unreservedly at him. You know you have created this insatiable ape-like appetite in them for male company, some rough and tumble; they can't get enough of it.

You would be so proud of their skiing. Otie thrives on the slopes without me – the moment I appear it all seems to go wrong. Theo's is quite solid now, which is reassuring given how hopeless I am. I would barely be able to rescue either of them, thank god you started them both so young. All these wonderful things you exposed them to . . . all I have to do is keep it going.

Easter Monday, 13th April

We went for a very quick ski this morning while the little ones watched a film. It was beautiful.

I went to pay our hotel bill and Charles had paid for all our drinks. He's so understated and genuinely kind.

Heading back home now. Oh god I miss our baby so so much!

I'm sitting waiting for our ride while the boys play. I keep seeing you around in your grey ski top which I would nestle into, your bigness, your tanned, windburnt cheekbones pointing up like the Alps themselves. I miss having you to whip your boys into shape, you all with your own games and secret language, which I only ever observed.

I think *The Kid* is going ahead, which would be amazing. I have work I must do if it does happen. I must also restart work on *The School Gate* before the production company completely loses interest. There are a few work, well, money-making opportunities around and an audition for a film I'm not overly excited about, but I can get myself there, because we need it. I need to put some money aside if I can into government bonds or something, make some interest, I want to set up a school fund. If I can maintain the house and set up a fund, it's enough, anything else is a bonus. We still have the cottage, which feels like a miracle. Maybe it is a crazy waste of money as it costs so much to run, but right now it feels such an integral part of your legacy. It's a little energy funnel/channel between you and the boys. I have to keep it for at least five years until Baby can really have memories of it too and then, if it's crippling us, well, we'll see . . .

Angel, you did so incredibly well to get a life policy. Robert Craig brilliantly navigated our way through the probate. Thank god Jane recommended him – I'm eternally grateful to her. I want to run around and tell everyone to get life policies, however small, and to make wills. I feel quite evangelical about it.

I'm recording all these diaries on to my computer now so that I don't forget or lose everything. I'm so slow at typing; it takes such a long time. I don't know if it's worth writing it all up and articulating any of these thoughts. Everything is just a phase, maybe this is to cement it in some way, to solidify something that should flow and change its course/current? I should write a fictional story instead or concentrate on finishing the series I started. I am glad you liked that – you read my first lame attempt at writing.

Something else I found in the C. S. Lewis book:

For in grief nothing 'stays put'. One keeps on emerging from a phase, but it always recurs. Round and round. Everything repeats. Am I going in circles or dare I hope I am on a spiral?

But if a spiral, am I going up or down it?

How often – will it be for always? – how often will the vast emptiness astonish me like a complete novelty and make me say, 'I never realised my loss till this moment?' The same leg is cut off time after time. The first plunge of the knife into the flesh is felt again and again.

It helps to read about grief, other people's, even news stories, other people's horrors, helps me – maybe I should share mine, do you think it could help someone else?

★

I have so much organising to do now, for the kids' summer arrangements, LA rental, schooling, camps, travel for everyone, etc. Will sign out and get on with responsibilities – I remember how surprised you always were at my keeping a diary so regularly. You never did, but then you filmed everything instead, thank god! We did have those 'holiday diaries' where I would write our impressions of a place and you would sketch them – do you remember that little red velvet notebook we had? You were such a 'doer' – what was the point of ever being retrospective about anything when you could just carry on and do more? I have to accept that difference between us. As much as I appreciate that energy in you, it can't be transferred to me. I would lose my bearing if I didn't constantly check back to view how my world was turning.

Bank holiday, 4th May

I cannot believe how long it is since I have written, three weeks? I find it harder and harder. It is both harder to let you go and harder to let you in at the same time. I miss you sorely and terribly if I allow myself.

We're in the cottage. I'm sitting in front of the huge poster invitation Tom Hammick made for your 40th birthday party (I have had it framed). I love it, your audacity, your spirit, your irrepressible spirit, your determination to extract everything out of life, live every breath so fully.

The boys (the big ones) are in equal measure amazing, loving, delicious and impossible, truculent, deaf to my every instruction – healthy and normal, I suppose. I wish you were here to help, love and guide them and to love me too. I miss your showering of love so much. I miss running out and getting you things, leaping on you, loving you, talking to you for hours and hours.

I was looking at pictures from our last big adventure to Mexico and Cuba and I remember so vividly us lying in our pool filled with lilies and chatting and you bargaining for another baby – convincing me what a great idea it would be. Well, thank god you convinced me. He has brightened our world immeasurably since you and somehow made it bearable for all of us.

5th May

Oh dear. I cried for the first time in a long while this morning. No, that's not true – I heaved a sob yesterday whilst jogging, but swallowed it back as there simply wasn't time for it. Thank god for tasks – even though I find them arduous and dull they wrench me back from the abyss of self-indulgence.

I've always believed in nurture over nature – I suppose I am hoping for the first time the balance might flip the other way. The boys are carrying large wads of your DNA around. I am now the sole 'nurturer' – please can you be the predominant gene force? – they will be getting too much of me already.

You had all the answers you know. Even when I chose not to listen to you, you had all the answers.

I want you back so much – when I let myself imagine the possibility of that, I can't breathe properly. It is such a physical response to a thought; my throat constricts and my eyes smart. I remember you used to use that expression 'eyes smarting', you said your love for me made your eyes smart. I never actually saw you cry, isn't that extraordinary? You said you couldn't recall the last time you had cried – when you were ten or eleven years old, you thought?

There is someone I keep wanting to call. It niggles me. I run through a mental list, someone who can get me closer to you again.

I think of Neil, your mother, one of your sisters perhaps? Someone who can shine some light on you when you are in reprieve like this. You are a shadow and if we all beam enough light on you maybe it will be like 'charging you up'; all of our collective thoughts and feelings for you might make your presence felt more. I then realise within twenty seconds or so of this inner dialogue that the person I want to call is you.

What a day it will be when I can no longer remember your phone number. Does that number already belong to someone else? They had better be using it to send love messages. You will be replaced little by little, at work, as a purchaser on Amazon (they must miss you a lot), as a band member, as a tennis partner, as a member of the mass of organisations you were involved in. Perhaps one day your role as a father and husband will be filled by another too. I can't help crying just thinking of that. You will never ever be replaced as a son, though, not even a part of you, utterly irreplaceable. But it is essential you are replaced, otherwise there will be these big gaping holes everywhere, OR must the holes remain, is that the point of loss, of missing, you get used to living with the craters? Not to acknowledge the person is missing is not to acknowledge they were ever there. Fears, all my fears, guilty fear – you were so free of all that crap.

You died 50 weeks ago. Another 50 weeks will distance us even more from when you were last here and there is absolutely *nothing* I can do about it.

I feel like a frantic, forgetful person in a room having lost a key, and unless I find it very quickly the key will no longer fit the lock.

I think, How can I have been so careless? How stupid of me. I've looked everywhere, even in the most unlikely places. I must replace it before I forget how to use it.

Love. Love is what I have lost and a part of me is frantic for that feeling again and yet repulsed, overwhelmed by the idea of trying to find it with someone else.

Strangely the room I imagine scavenging around in to find 'the missing thing' is my own first bedroom. It had wallpaper with chirping birds all over it and the sound of crashing waves outside the windows. It smelt slightly clammy, the air heavy with sea salt and had a fluffy caramel carpet underfoot to compensate.

So, we do regress in times of stress.

6th May

Oh it's your birthday tomorrow. I know you never cared about that, but I do now. You will not be a year older; your watch has stopped.

While Theo was having a bath last night, he was looking at the collage of you and them. He started to talk about the possibility of you coming back. He conceded it was 99% impossible but that left a 1% of possibility. He thought about it for a while and then said to me, 'You know nothing is IMpossible.' I feel so happy writing to you, speaking to you in this way. It is like coming home.

I am looking through drawers of old diaries where I keep pictures of you, letters and drawings. I found a faxed page covered in your cartoons. You had drawn a cartoon of 'our world', made one half of the page a cartoon of me and the other half a sketch of you and then a series of pipes connecting us and speech bubbles as to how and why. Anyway, there listed in the column of things I should pursue, 'write' was at the top. I must always listen to your advice – how did you know it would comfort me so much? I must go back over my diaries if I ever have the time and rake through them for nuggets of wisdom and insight from you. Looking at these things creates a fresh surge of yearning. I want to lay it all to rest, yet I can't, as the stronger urge is still to stagger through life like a somnambulist, remaining in a dream with you. I was in the studio at the top of the house, the sun was shining through the skylights and it reminded me of the heat I felt, the sun beating down on my pregnant body when I received that most dreadful phone call. No, it didn't *remind* me of that – it was more like a sense memory, a shock, a syringe full of horror.

You always said to me, say yes to everything until it becomes abundantly clear that the answer should be no – or words to that effect.

I am trying very hard to do that.

'Work hard. Expect nothing. Celebrate!'

I will walk through doors rather than waiting tentatively at the thresholds.

10th May

I am about to land in New York to do a quick screen test. I think this is the quickest trip I will have ever made here. I'll be in Manhattan for a few hours. I am not mad about the project. What's the point of this carbon footprint?

I wish I had you to call and tell about this as I used to. Remarkably you never seemed to tire of it. You always wanted to know everything, the smallest detail. I miss that kind of sharing – without it there are holes everywhere. Baby, I don't know if I was ever bored by you, well maybe I'd drift off when you would talk about the power of Led Zeppelin or the wonder of a Jimi Hendrix solo, but apart from that I pretty much hung on your every word. Perhaps it was just the way you spoke. I loved listening to you, watching your mouth, the way it moved and tripped over itself, the words getting trapped between your big lips, stuck on their way out. I remember you used to say you had lips like a dingy, a luscious life raft more like . . . The way you viewed the world, this experience, it was peering through a new kaleidoscope for me.

I remember once when I had to go to Paris to test for a movie. I was probably under-prepared. I had just had Beanie and was squeezing into a skirt and trying to find things to wear to mask my overflowing boobs.

It was already a huge wrench leaving him behind. I had fed him, packed the pump, hopped on the train to do the test, then would get back to London in time for the last feed. When I arrived, there were about fourteen people in the room, no hellos just a 'which page do you want to start on?'. Arghhh! I wanted to run . . . milk was rising . . . I pulled a scarf out of my bag and whipped it round my neck to hang down and cover the milk leaks appearing through my shirt. I didn't make it, I was useless; I didn't have a clue. I felt trippy and just wanted to be released from the agony of a bad audition. But no, they wanted more:

'Come on, just try it one more time,' as I continued to slip and slide and spin off-piste. When I left the room, my toes curled firmly up, a lump rose in my throat. Was it separation from Beanie, hormones? Not sure I shoved it back down and ran for the train.

I remember flopping into my seat feeling so relieved it was over because I had you and this tiny creature we had created. I just longed to be back in your arms. The job, or now lack of, would just be flushed away in an instant. I had you and my newborn baby – there would be other jobs.

You came to collect me from the Eurostar with tiny Bean in his car seat and you had placed a bouquet of flowers across him and wrapped his still skinny arms around them so it looked as if he had bought them himself. Those kinds of gestures, they were effortless for you – you never looked for approval, you simply followed your impulse and then carried on. I remember allowing my eyes to well up as you clasped me tight. Nestled in his car seat, which was dangling from your hand, our tiny creation peered up like an owlette. His daddy could take care of everything. How lucky were we?

Monday 11th May

We're going to land at Heathrow shortly. I grabbed a few hours of shifty sleep. I was thinking of you as I opened my gritty eyes, your contact lenses on long flights, having to blink yourself awake, your lips puffed up like big cushions I could sink mine into. I thought we would go on and on, you were my person, where I lived, we made a habitat together and we put some pups in it. The roof is off now and we're all exposed.

Oh, Twinx, I miss our language, all the substitute words, secret codes, humour buried everywhere like little treasures between rocks. I write to you like this to be with you for a few moments, to smell what's left of you. You were glamour, real glamour, the kind that ripples through a room and leaves everyone affected. How did you become all that? How did all these qualities assimilate in one person?

I was occasionally told by other people that you had changed a great deal since we had been together. You used to say, 'You have improved me so much.' I just hope you died knowing how much you had transformed me over our years together. I had, and still have, a hell of a way to go, but you cracked open so much for me.

I am slowly now accepting that we have one short life, when I had always thought I had all the time in the world. I could just stand waiting in the wings with a sack of ideas and no courage to live them. You have given me the courage. I know they say we can't be changed by another, but you have changed me. Your example is one I want to follow, what a relief that something is left, thank you for everything, for this experience of loving.

After school p/up

Theo is sitting next to me doing his maths homework whilst we wait for Otie to finish football club. I am extremely proud of him. He came second in the junior chess championships having barely played since you died. He is such wonderful company, you know. Oh god, you're missing all the best bits . . .

19th May

It's Beanie's actual birthday today. I woke up very early with a huge weight on my chest. I remembered back to the day he was born – the look on your face as you held him. There was joy, pure joy, awe, but also vulnerability and a terror that I had never seen in you before. I loved you so much in that moment. How amazing was all of that? Going back to our red lacquered house without a clue of what to do with this little Bean.

Beanie then wandered into my room as I was shoving these memories away, this remarkable little boy who is nine! How? He had already dressed but he climbed back into my bed for the hugest hug and became my small brown-eyed doe again. I know we both lay there thinking, *Maybe*, waiting for something to happen as it was his birthday . . .

20th May

I had a flare of hope, a flash of excitement, as I wrote that date. Am I expecting you to come back and read all this one day? Read all the bits of life you have missed, being away this last year?

The boys wrote the most amazing speeches about you last night and this morning. Otie only turned six a week ago (didn't tell you, but he had his friends to sleepover too and we erected a kind of circus tent in the top studio – he was SO proud). There is nothing 'flaky' about him. He's so solid, already so sure of who he is right now. Anyway, he wrote his own speech to you, got tired writing so then dictated the rest for me to write on a document on my computer while he perched on my lap wide-eyed, watching his words come to life on the screen. I can't tell you how proud you would be. It's a mad thing to say, but it is a privilege to be mother to these boys.

At least I still live on in this world we created together, in the eye of it, that's a family, three boys and me – might that be enough?

I went to admire your gravestone again this morning and the one just along from yours belongs to a little child and her parents had had engraved:

'All that we have loved deeply becomes a part of us.'

I am beginning to believe this is true. I love you. I want to feel, touch and hold you, share everything with you. I will speak about you tonight – we shall celebrate you!

★

Here's what I said about you. I would love more to put down what the boys said, but I feel it's their property now. I've put the speeches in their memory boxes.

I know Norman and others will speak ABOUT you tonight, but as I sit down I find I can still only write TO you. I think I ended up doing that at your 40th – I stood up to talk about you and ended up talking straight to you much to your embarrassment.

I can't believe you won't be embarrassed any more. It all seems that much more finite when I break your absence down into the specifics of what you can and can no longer 'do' or 'be'. No one can be more enraged by your death than you. Your tenacity has been snipped like a thread – how dare that happen? How could it? As Theo said to me, 'I just don't understand where that heart attack came from.'

I can't believe it's a year ago that I sat at my desk with a window of thirty minutes from the kids to write you a letter that I would put in your coffin. We made a little casket stuffed with your favourite books, CDs and messages of love.

A funeral, it's such a crazy, ridiculous thing after a sudden, unexpected death. How could I possibly collect a thought, access a memory or summarise your life thus far when I expected it to continue for another forty years? It felt so cheap, scribbling things down off the top of my head. All I did know was how much I completely and utterly loved you, every square inch of you, inside and out. You were exceptional.

From here on I feel I can't let myself love you any more. I have to try to fold the love up, put it in a box, another precious casket, because it's just too bloody painful. Nothing, nothing, will ever be forgotten about you, but I can't haul these images of you, words from you, around in my head forever, because, just as you did, they take up all my acreage. I have to find a storage space where I can occasionally go and lift all the lids off and stare in wonder at what we had, and accept that word 'had'.

How does one do that? End a relationship that has never ended? What does that mean, a year on? I've been clutching this balloon, this beautiful tight balloon which is you, your spirit, our love, and I'm letting go of the string. I'm watching it disappear into the sky. It is terrifying but necessary I think.

We have this seven-month-old baby boy who you'll never meet, but you made him. Thank god I had you there to usher Theo and Otis into the world so beautifully. It's as if you'd given me so much love then that there was enough left over to help me push this one out (into the world too). I couldn't have done it if I hadn't had those first experiences with you.

His name is Rex Coltrane and he doesn't stop smiling. He seems to know life is just there to be sucked up, inhaled and enjoyed. He grips on to me, pedals his legs with such enthusiasm, desperate to get going, to begin his journey. I've always thought it was very soppy when people used to go on about how children teach you so much. I'd sceptically think, yes, they teach you patience. Well, I'm humbled by him. His irrepressible joy has given me untold happiness. As have Theo and Otis – they are everything you would want them to be. I've been following them this last year, resting in their shadows. They have such energy, a constant hunger for new experiences, zeal that squeals so loudly and a huge capacity to love. What can I say? They are most definitely their father's sons.

Theo said the other day, 'I think Rex has replaced Dadu. Isn't it strange that someone so tiny who can't do anything can replace someone so big who could do everything?'

Otis said shortly after you died, 'It's okay. Dadu isn't dead. He's just rocking out up in heaven!'

It's been the strangest life since you died, ricocheting between a belief that I'll fail them, not live up to all our dreams and then sudden bursts of conviction that I can and will do everything and they will all thrive – the reality is somewhere in between, I think.

Grief, in all its agony, has these moments of luminosity. I realised today I've often been on a high from grief. It's like falling in love – an absurd notion, but the feelings nestle side by side: my grief for you is also my love for you fighting for its last few breaths.

There's nothing to say; you're not here. I still can't trace that back to its beginning like most other facts, but you are not.

This memorial, it's to remember you, so us who loved you will follow your example and live life like there's no tomorrow, live it for ourselves and with one another and not in your memory any more. You'd be appalled by that. You leave so many 'affected' people behind, you would be shocked. You lived your life in such detail, so much accuracy, colour and rhythm. I hope I can remember it all.

Two last things — I actually have no place to speak on behalf of these people but since they could not be here perhaps I can pass on my impression . . .

I took our sons to meet your father for the first time. I know you wanted this and it never quite happened, but now it's done and it was beautiful.

It ended up being an incredibly charmed and harmonious day.

And then your mother — my god, what a woman! I love her because she loves you so much. I can't ever begin to imagine what it would be like to have my son die before me. I don't think I'd be able to stand up, let alone walk and run as she has been doing. You would be so proud of her. In one of our many tearful conversations she said, 'I can't come. I don't care how great he was or what he achieved, he's just my son. He could have been a criminal for all I care. The point is he's gone. He was just too good to be true.'

Anyway, I love you, I always will, and here's two messages from your cubs who along with their brother will continue to grow up — their courage to keep growing so strong without you here. I must say, it would take your breath away . . .

21st May

Hello, angel, here we are again on a transatlantic flight in the middle of someone's night and I am thinking about you. So it didn't work — the anniversary being a wave breaking and you dissolving into foam, dissipating.

I'm glad.

Acknowledgements

My thanks to the unsung heroines in my life:
Sophie, Veronika, Isabel
and Maggie.

A percentage of the proceeds from the sale of this book will be donated to Facing the World, a children's charity set up by Martin and other leading British craniofacial surgeons. The charity offers facial reconstructive surgery to children from Third World countries whose lives are blighted by disfigurement. For more information on Facing the World go to www.facingtheworld.co.uk.

Notes to quotations

p.13 'Martin' by Adam Searle.

p.16 'When sorrows come . . .' from *Hamlet*, IV.v.87–98.

p.55 '. . . the tender soles of the feet . . .' from *The Earthly Paradise* by William Morris.

p.56 'Love set you going . . .' from 'Morning Song' from *Ariel* by Sylvia Plath, reproduced by kind permission of Faber & Faber, © 1968, Faber & Faber.

p.59 'You have taken the east from me' from 'Donal Og' (Young Donald) by Anonymous, tr. Lady Augusta Gregory.

p.77 'When we get out of the glass bottles of our own ego' from 'Escape' by D. H. Lawrence.

p.83 'Still, there's no denying . . .' from *A Grief Observed* by C. S. Lewis, © 1966 Faber & Faber.

p.92 'Soldier, scholar, horseman, he . . .' from 'In Memory of Major Robert Gregory' by W. B. Yeats.

p.99 'For in grief . . .' from *A Grief Observed* by C. S. Lewis, © 1966 Faber & Faber.